Berlin Blockade

D1599800

Berlin Blockade

John Man

Editor-in-Chief: Barrie Pitt
Editor: David Mason
Art Director: Sarah Kingham
Picture Editor: Robert Hunt
Consultant Art Editor: Denis Piper
Designer: David Allen
Illustration: John Batchelor/David Penney
Photographic Research: Carina Dvorak
Cartographer: Richard Natkiel

Photographs for this book were especially selected from the following archives:
Camera Press, London; Suddeutscher Verlag, Munich; Novosti, London;
Staatsbibliothek, Berlin; Black Star, London; Keystone, London; Ullstein,
Berlin; Associated Press, London; United Press International, London.

First Printing: July 1973
Printed in United States of America

Ballantine Books Inc.
201 East 50th Street
New York, N.Y. 10022

Contents

Island in a communist sea

Introduction by Lieutenant-Colnel A. J. Barker

At the same time, however, the Russians started to create a new German army (initially disguised as 'people's police'), and the West responded in the form of the NATO-integrated *Bundeswehr*. All this was a direct result of the Berlin blockade, which turned the process of re-building German industrial might into a race between the two power blocs.

East Germany emerged as a nominally independent member of the Soviet satellite system. But the Russians had no hope of matching the rising standard of living in the Federal Republic, because the West controlled the bigger and traditionally more industrialized part of the country. Economic difficulties in East Germany, propagated by the imposition of measures to further 'socialism', led to an increase in the numbers of refugees going West. This in turn increased the strains and stresses of East German life and produced yet more refugees. A Soviet ultimatum, amounting to a demand that the West should recognize the *Deutsche Demokratische Republik* of East Germany or suffer more interference with their position in Berlin, further contributed to the outflow of people from East Germany. When it was clear that the West were not going to submit to a strategy of blackmail over Berlin, the Eastern part of the city was sealed off from the Western sectors and the Berlin Wall was built.

The Wall is a scar bisecting a great city. It is physically ugly and morally uglier still. Since 13th August 1961, when construction first began, the initial barbed wire fencing has been strengthened and replaced several times, each wall being more escape-proof than the last. West Berliners have learned to live with the Wall, although they do not accept it. Since the Four Power Agreement on Berlin of September 1971 came into force in June 1972, West Berliners have made two-and-a-half million visits to the East. (In 1972 there was also a 30 per cent increase in escapes from the East into the West, with 1,245 East Germans slipping directly into West Germany or West Berlin.) But it is easier to get garbage across the Wall than people,. for despite agreement many West Berliners are still reluctant to visit the East. East Berlin, where the guards change to the goose step, is a dreary place even if the Communists did manage to grab the most important museums and theatres. Because there is little commercial life and no gaiety, the West Berliners have come to believe that the harassment and humiliation to which they are subjected at the border is just not worth the trip. They are now overtly resigned to being an island for ever. Their very existence constantly re-states the dream of a re-united Germany but very few feel it will ever come about.

Meanwhile life in West Berlin continues its peculiar way. The Allied Powers who guarantee the city's freedom and military security are a constant irritant to national sensitivities but West Berliners know that the troops of the United States, Britain and France are a necessary embarrassment without which they would be over-run. The threat of a repeat of the 1948-49 blockade is always on people's minds: there is always the Wall to remind them of it. Other cities have been reduced to rubble and ashes and have risen anew. But only Berlin had the doubtful distinction of being resuscitated to become one of the storm centres of international conflict. Since 1945 the West's steadfast refusal to withdraw from Berlin and to recognize the communist regime of East Germans as the legitimate government of a sovereign state has been one of the most visible manifestations of the struggle between two irreconcilable philosophies of life: communist regimentation and democratic freedom. Crisis after crisis has been fabricated by the Communists in their attempts to 'settle' the Berlin problem on Soviet terms, and the confrontation of 1948 took the world to the very brink of a conflict which could have ended in a nuclear holocaust.

At the height of the crisis numerous and not always insignificant voices were raised, arguing that Berlin was not worth fighting for. Berlin is not essential to the defence of Europe, they said; give it to the Russians and the trouble will all be over. Such pleas have been repeated many times since 1948, and from the purely military point of view they are right: Berlin *is* militarily untenable. As a tiny island in a communist sea, it is a military absurdity, and the West would actually gain from consolidating its defence line by abandoning Berlin. But what the advocates of appeasement overlook or ignore is that it is the political symbolism of Berlin, and not its military significance, which makes the holding of the city's Western sectors imperative.

In 1945 the four-power occupation of Berlin became a symbol of the joint victory over Nazi Germany by the major powers of the West and the East. The initial four-power cooperation in Berlin became the symbol of mankind's hopes for a joint building of a better world. Unfortunately, the East-West honeymoon was short and utterly disappointing. Berlin served as a barometer for the rapidly changing political climate. As Moscow proceeded to force communist regimes on all the east and central European nations, tensions in Berlin grew until the city became the symbol of a rapidly crystallizing division of the world between the communist East and the democratic West Three years after the end of the war the process was essentially completed and the West – by then almost demobilized – had to make the painful choice between opposing further Soviet expansion or abandoning its hard-won share of victory over Nazism to another ruthless dictatorship. The decision was made when the Communists grabbed Czechoslovakia in early 1948. And when Stalin tried to grab Berlin a few months later, the divided city became the symbol of this decision to oppose Soviet aggressiveness. The air lift, the formation of NATO and, later on, the costly defence of South Korea all stemmed from this decision.

The airlift enabled Berlin to survive. It also radically altered the relationship between Germany and the Western Allies from that between occupiers and occupied to something approaching partnership in a joint enterprise. In effect, therefore, the Russians succeeded in furthering the very measures of Western consolidation which the blockade had been designed to check. When they realized this, Soviet policy towards Germany was drastically and dramatically altered. The blockade was called off, while a peace offensive and a campaign for German unity was mounted.

Thin edge of
the wedge

Berlin, 1945: 'As far as you can see in all directions from the plane above the city, a great wilderness of debris dotted with roofless burnt out buildings that look like little mouse traps with low autumn sun shining through the spaces where windows had been.' Thus wrote the eminent war correspondent William Shirer, as he flew into the German capital a few days after the end of the war. 'Most of the little streets I knew gone, erased off the map, railroad stations . . . gaunt shells, the imperial palace of the Kaisers – roofless, some of its wings pulverised and here and there the outer walls battered in.'

It didn't seem much of a prize in material terms, but it was the focal point both of Allied strategy towards the end of the war and for those who had, since 1943, been planning the face of post-war Europe.

The city had tremendous political and psychological significance. Pre-war Berlin was in area the world's largest city, and had the fourth largest population; it had been the leading political and cultural centre of Central Europe, the heart of its greatest single industrial complex – at the height of Hitler's empire – of most of Europe.

Berlin thus played a central part in the war-time Allied discussions on the administration of the country and its capital after victory. It was decided that the land should be divided into three occupation zones – a plan devised by Clement Attlee, British Deputy Prime Minister in 1943 – with the Russians in the East, the British in the North-West and the Americans in the South-West. This was embodied in an agreement signed on 14th November 1944, in London, which set up an Allied Control Council to administer occupied Germany with the four commanders-in-chief acting in concert. In early 1945, when these arrangements were confirmed by the four powers at Yalta, the French were

The Reichstag in Berlin in 1945

9

also given a zone, carved out of the American and British ones.

The agreement gave Russia present day East Germany, and Berlin was 110 miles inside it. If this seems over generous, it should be remembered that Russia was bearing the brunt of the struggle against Germany at this stage. The Allied invasion of Normandy was still several months off.

It was also agreed that the city of Berlin should be administered independently of any of the zones of occupation and that it should be divided into sectors, each to be occupied by one of the Allied powers.

The question of Western Allied access to Berlin, of enormous subsequent significance, was never discussed; relations with Russia during the war were precarious anyway and to insist on such apparent technicalities might have seemed like a confession of bad faith. The American ambassador to Britain, John Winnant, stated the accepted Western view when he said that he believed: 'that the right to be in Berlin carried with it the right of access' (Clay: *Decision in Germany*) and to insist on its inclusion in an agreement on the division of Germany after the war 'would arouse Soviet suspicion and make mutual understanding more difficult to attain'. Besides, it was generally understood that when the zones were established they would not be sealed off one from another. Even with the end of the war in sight, when the Allies met at Yalta in early 1945, Russian reluctance to discuss the question of access was enough to get the matter dropped. No significance was attached to the Russian attitude.

An interesting fact concerning the way these crucial decisions were arrived at emerges from the documents. At one stage President Roosevelt had rejected out of hand

Pre-war Berlin, nerve center of Nazism

11

Clement Attlee, who proposed the division of post-war Germany into three occupation zones

Attlee's proposals. He wanted the Russian zone to stop level with Berlin, and the Americans to have occupation of the north of Germany, thus giving them access from the sea. Due to lack of co-ordination, however, and confusion over areas of responsibility in the American administration, his wishes were not passed on in time to the American representatives actually hammering out the agreement on post-war Germany in London. Had this been done, the boundaries might have been drawn quite differently and the subsequent history of Berlin, of Germany and of all Western Europe might have been totally different.

In June 1944, with the Allies advancing from the west, Eisenhower named Berlin as the Chief Allied Objective, a policy befitting the city's importance.

The 'Big Three' at Yalta

General Eisenhower

He soon changed his mind, for what afterwards appeared to be a very odd reason. The American command had become increasingly preoccupied with the supposed need to occupy Bavaria, the original home, the 'National Redoubt', of Nazism. American military leaders were convinced by intelligence reports that the powers which had hitherto guided Germany would survive in the south to re-organise her resurrection. In conformity with this belief, General Bedell Smith told a press conference in April 1945, 'from a purely military standpoint Berlin does not have much significance any more'. But the 'National Redoubt' idea was all, of course, nonsense, as became clear at the end of the war.

There were other reasons, too, for not going for Berlin. The advance would come under the command of Montgomery – hardly a popular move with the Americans who were eager for their own victories, and it might

Field-Marshal Montgomery

Lesen und weitergeben!

Der Panzerbär

26. April 1945

KAMPFBLATT FÜR DIE VERTEIDIGER GROSS-BERLINS

Die Schlacht auf dem Höhepunkt
Deutsche Reserven im Eilmarsch auf Berlin

Seit 2½ Monaten rennen die Sowjets gegen Breslau an

Aus dem Führerhauptquartier, 25. April

Das Oberkommando der Wehrmacht gibt bekannt:

Beiderseits der unteren Weser und im Frontbogen zwischen dem Küstenkanal und Delmenhorst behaupteten sich unsere Divisionen bei geringem Geländeverlust gegen alle Durchbruchsversuche der Engländer und Kanadier.

Von der Weser südöstlich Bremen bis zur Elbe bei Horneburg hielten die schweren Abwehrkämpfe mit gleicher Stärke an. Zäh Widerstand leistend, behaupteten unsere Verbände ihre Stellungen. Die Stadt Horneburg wurde wiedergenommen.

In der Schlacht um Berlin wird um jeden Fußbreit Boden gerungen. Im Süden drangen die Sowjets bis in die Linie Babelsberg — Zehlendorf — Neukölln vor. Im östlichen und nördlichen Stadtgebiet dauern heftige Straßenkämpfe an. Westlich der Stadt erreichten sowjetische Panzerspitzen den Raum von Nauen und Ketzin. Nordwestlich Oranienburg wird das Nordufer des Ruppiner Kanals gegen starke Angriffe gehalten. Wiederholte Vorstöße auf Eberswalde führten zu Einbrüchen im südlichen Stadt...

durch den Vorstoß starker feindlicher Infanterie- und Panzerverbände zwischen Reggio und Ferrara an den Po verlagert. Die Angriffe der 5. amerikanischen Armee im ligurischen Küstenabschnitt und im westetrurischen Apennin blieben in der Masse vor unseren Gebirgsstellungen liegen.

Starke kommunistische Bandenkräfte haben sich in dem unwegsamen Gebirgsgelände Nordwestdalmatiens bis in den Raum Fiume vorgeschoben und stehen im Stadtrand im Kampf mit unserer Besatzung.

Im Südabschnitt der Ostfront hält die Lage weiterhin gefestigt. Der Schwerpunkt der Kämpfe lag gestern bei Brünn, wo die Bolschewisten einen tieferen Einbruch erzielten. Nordwestlich Mäh-

risch-Ostrau wurden erneute Durchbruchsversuche des Feindes zerschlagen.

Feind befreit. Die Bolschewisten hatten in diesen Kämpfen sehr hohe blutige Verluste, umfangreiche Beute wurde gebracht.

An der Oderfront griff der Gegner aus seinem Brückenkopf nördlich Gartz unter starkem Artillerie- und Schlachtfliegereinsatz an und konnte bis in den Raum westlich Tantow vorstoßen. Weiter nördlich wurden wiederholte Angriffe in gutem Zusammenwirken mit unserer Artillerie zerschlagen.

Auf der Landzunge von Pillau errangen unsere Verbände in schweren Waldkämpfen erneute Abwehrerfolge.

Vor der westnorwegischen Küste brachten Sicherungsfahrzeuge der Kriegsmarine neun britische Jagd-

bomber zum Absturz. Bei Tage warfen schwächere Kampfverbände Bomben im süd-

Freikorps Mohnke ruft!
Männer von Berlin!

In dieser Stunde der letzten großen Entscheidung im Kampf um Berlin gibt es wie immer in der deutschen Geschichte fanatische Einzelkämpfer, die mehr tun wollen als ihre Pflicht, die sich dem verhaßten Feind mit allen Mitteln entgegenwerfen wollen, um ihm heimzuzahlen, was er an Leid und Tod, an Unglück und Zerstörung über unser Volk und über unsere Stadt gebracht hat.

Auch Ihr gehört dazu!

Auch Ihr habt den unbändigen Willen, einen letzten entscheidenden Gegenschlag gegen die in Berlin eingedrungenen Bolschewisten an erster Stelle zu stehen! Euer Platz ist im Freikorps Mohnke!

Das Freikorps Mohnke stellt kampfbereite und entschlossene Männer sofort ein!

Leuchtend zeigt es sich jetzt in der höchsten Gefahr, wer ein anständiger Kerl ist und das Herz auf dem rechten Fleck hat, wer keinen Einsatz scheut und treu zur selbstgewählten Fahne steht!

Niemals haben wir uns dem Führer mehr verbunden gefühlt als in dieser Stunde, in der er sich entschied, unter uns zu bleiben, mit uns zu kämpfen und den Feind zu schlagen.

Es lebe der Führer!

Ein Hundsfott, wer in dieser Stunde die schimpfliche Feigheit dem männlichen Kampfe vorzieht

---

The last propaganda news-sheet to encourage the defenders of Berlin

also cost tens of thousands of Allied lives. 'A pretty stiff price to pay', said General Omar Bradley, 'for a prestige objective, especially when we have got to fall back and let the othe fellow take over'.

In addition the Americans had, at this stage, an almost childlike faith in the goodwill of Russia. When it became clear that Germany would fall,

the need to preserve Allied solidarity came to dominate American thinking. Roosevelt said of Stalin: 'I think that if I give him everything I possibly can, he will work with me for a world of democracy and peace'.

For all these reasons Berlin was to be abandoned to the Russians while the Western Allies advanced only as far as the river Elbe.

Churchill was against the scheme. He told Roosevelt: 'nothing will exert a psychological effect of despair

14

upon all German forces of resistance equal to the fall of Berlin', and he added with prophetic insight, 'the Russian armies will, no doubt, overrun all of Austria and enter Vienna. If they also take Berlin, will not their impression that they have been the overwhelming contributor to our common victory be unduly printed on their minds and may this not lead them into a mood which will raise grave and formidable difficulties in the future?'

His objections had no effect. Eisenhower, who had already confirmed his policies with Stalin direct, had his decision confirmed in Washington and, since the Americans in Europe outnumbered the British three to one, Churchill backed down

Historic meeting on the Elbe between between American and Russian troops

with a laconic comment: 'To prove my sincerity', he said, 'I will use one of my very few Latin quotations: *Amanteum irae amoris integratio est.*' (Lovers' quarrels are a part of love.) As a result of the decision, when German resistance collapsed and the Americans found themselves on the Elbe just fifty-three miles from Berlin – about the same distance as the Russians were the other side of the city – they marked time for almost two weeks waiting for the Russians to advance.

Since the war Eisenhower has often been blamed for allowing the balance of power to be established in such an

Street scene in Berlin during the Red Army occupation; the Russians regarded all German property as lawful booty

unsatisfactory way. This is unfair on two counts: first, his designated task was to destroy Germany's armed forces, a purely military exercise which he performed to the best of his ability uncomplicated by political considerations; and second, even if he had believed with Montgomery that 'War is a political instrument', and plunged on to Berlin and taken the city, the situation would not have been much different. The zones of occupation had been agreed in advance and such an act would almost certainly have made relations with the Russians even more difficult.

Despite the vociferous objections of Churchill and Montgomery, therefore, the Russians were allowed to be the first to reach Berlin.

At dawn on 16th April 1945, a stupefying artillery barrage presaged the Russian crossing of the Oder, and on 2nd May they took Berlin. The next few days were a period of terror

Fierce street fighting developed when the Russians entered Berlin

for Berliners. Marauding Red soldiery went on an orgy of destruction and rape. A single Berlin hospital treated 230 rape victims in one day. The Russian troops had been told that everything was their lawful booty and they seized whatever they could lay their hands on: watches, fountain pens, flashlights, radios, light bulbs, toilet fixtures, drugs, food, machinery, refrigerators, kitchen utensils. For two months after the fall of Berlin the Russians had the city to themselves and they used the time well. Moscow, also, regarded Germany as the key to the balance of political power in Europe and planned to place the country as much as possible under communist control as a bridgehead from which their creed could spread over Europe. They were encouraged when, despite Churchill's expressions of horror, America decided to abandon

20,000 square miles in the previously agreed Eastern Sector and retreat to the zonal border, 110 miles west of Berlin. The Russian's next step was to bring Berlin thoroughly into the communist sphere. There was no-one to stop them; the idea of a 'communist threat' had not yet taken hold in Washington, and the recent withdrawal demonstrated how unconcerned America's leaders were to use military advantage to achieve political advantage.

Within those first two months the city government was largely given over to German communists. The head of the new police force was an ex-Nazi Officer, Paul Markgraf, who had been captured by the Russians at Stalingrad and indoctrinated as a communist. The banks, the trade union structure, the two newspapers and the radio station were all in communist hands. All four political parties were given permission to publish a newspaper but the Communist Party was the only one that received enough newsprint to do so. Wavering officials were bribed into loyalty with better rations – 2,485 calories a day, for instance, for politicians, party officials and teachers, as against 1,248 per day – almost starvation – at the lowest level, to which the unco-operative could easily be assigned.

When the Western Allies arrived they found an efficient city government operating amidst the shattered city described by William Shirer. The fact that it was communist controlled was not at first obvious and did not seem important. The Russians were still seen as noble allies in the cause of peace and freedom, and certainly at a superficial level they were friendly enough. There were many parties at which prodigious quantities of vodka were drunk. American GIs were able to supply Russian soldiers, rich with specially printed Occupation Marks, with otherwise unobtainable

The conquerors

Paul Markgraf

consumer goods.

Naturally enough it was the Germans who were regarded as enemies. It was to be some time before the Western Allies came to see the Germans as friends and the Russians as the true enemy.

Political warfare was likewise far removed from the minds of the Berliners themselves. Their country was broken: it had no government, no mail, no telephones for civil use; seven million of their countrymen had surrendered and were prisoners; four million refugees straggled across the land. The Berliners themselves huddled in broken homes behind cardboard-covered windows, two or three families to an apartment. Very many spent much of their time clearing rubble, having no other occupation. Thousands more streamed out of the city, carrying a few pitiful possessions in an aimless escape into

19

Russian HQ in Berlin in 1945

the countryside. Hospitals had few drugs. Dead bodies lay rotting in canals and bomb sites. In one borough of 14,000 houses only half were even habitable. The Russian printed currency had reduced Berlin's economy to a farce and it was totally dependent on the black market. The principal coin was the cigarette, one of which had a market value of about 50p Sterling or 1.25 US dollars. The murder rate had risen from about forty per year to well over 500.

One story that was universally believed tellingly reveals the mental state of the Berliners themselves. It concerns a blind man who bumped into a girl in the street; the girl apologised and asked if she could help the man in any way. Yes, she could: 'I have to deliver this letter', he said, 'but I have walked miles and I am very tired, 'could you deliver it for me?' The girl looked at the address; by good chance it was just a few streets away. She agreed to deliver it, but as she went on her way she chanced to look back and saw the blind man delivering another letter to another girl, presumably with the same story.

The no-fraternisation order is dutifully observed.

She went to the police who raided the apartment on the address and found two men and a woman and a quantity of meat which turned out to be human flesh. The girl was supposedly to have been the next victim.

This story was heard by many correspondents from many different sources but no evidence was ever found to support it. It gained such wide credence because such events seemed not unlikely in the bizarre conditions of occupied Berlin.

While the Berliners eked out their day to day existence the Western Allies tried to co-operate with the Russians. Their task was to establish the government of Germany on a regular basis and to agree a date for the Western Allied forces to enter Berlin. From the first it was tough. 5th June was set for the first meeting of the Allied Control Council in Berlin. The Russians proved recalcitrant. General Grigori Zhukov kept the other three Commanders-in-Chief waiting for hours in their apartments and only appeared when threatened with the abandonment of the meeting.

21

Left: These whose houses were not completely destroyed considered themselves lucky. Above: Many spent their days clearing rubble. Below: A quiet dance during a break

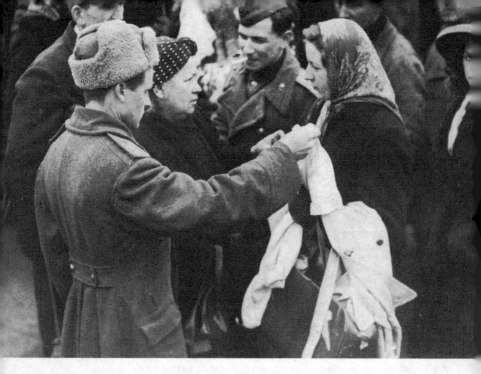

Above and Below: Black market activities. *Right:* The harsh reality of day to day existence: a Berliner hopes to find edible scraps among discarded fruit skins.

General Lucius Clay

He had objected to a provision in the draft that would have required Russia to arrest Japanese citizens in Russia, clearly an error since the two countries were not then at war. When the offending clause was deleted, the meeting proceeded. General Montgomery recalled later, in somewhat impatient words: 'I was so fed up with the whole affair that I suggested the offending word be deleted from the text; this suggestion was at once agreed to by the Russians and by everyone else, and to this day I do not know what difference it made'.

The Russians then refused to discuss any further matters except to agree to the setting up of a Governing Committee, or *Kammandatura*, for Berlin until the Western Allies agreed to remove their troops from the eastern zone.

Three weeks later, at a new meeting, this was agreed as the first item on the agenda. The Western delegates were then expecting to discuss arrangements for formal access to Berlin. But, as Churchill had feared, the West

Opening of the Allied Control Council; left to right, Montgomery, Zhukov, Eisenhower and Lattre de Tassigny

Refugees seek a freer life in the West

had lost its trump card with the promised withdrawal of its troops. Marshal Zhukov, a short, heavy-set, humourous man who wielded his power with practiced ease, stated baldly that he considered access to be a privilege, not a right. The West could use one road, one railway and an air corridor, with the use of Gatow and Tempelhof – the two airports in the Western Sector of Berlin. He was hard to resist: a marshal of the Soviet Union, Russia's greatest war hero, he clearly outranked his opposite numbers, General Clay – Eisenhower's deputy as Military Governor and the man who was to be the dominant personality during the airlift – and Lieutenant General Sir Ronald Weeks, Montgomery's deputy. They nevertheless demurred and Zhukov, with a show of magnanimity, said that the arrangement might be considered a temporary one, at which both Clay and Weeks agreed.

The agreement was not a written one. As Clay stated later, 'We didn't wish to accept specific routes which might be interpreted as a denial of our right of access over all routes'. Nothing was recorded about the Russian's right to impose border controls and Clay, to his later mortification, merely assumed that access would be free. As a result of this agreement the United States and Britain began to withdraw their forces on 1st July 1945, followed by a mass of refugees and others seeking safety from the Red Army. In the words of Winston Churchill: 'Soviet Russia was established in the heart of Europe. This was a fateful milestone for mankind.' By hindsight, of course, it was a mistake to withdraw Allied troops, but few suspected the intransigence the Russians were to show and the West, still eager to display its willingness to co-operate, complied with Russian demands.

Scene in a West Berlin refugee camp

29

Technical difficulties

Following the Russian closure of a bridge 'for repairs', civilians are obliged to cross the Elbe by ferry

Colonel Frank Howley, who later became Commandant of the American Sector in Berlin, described the scene as the American forces thrust down the autobahn to Berlin: 'On July 1st 1945, the road to Berlin was the high road to bedlam. It was packed with tanks, trucks and other vehicles . . . all hurrying towards the previously forbidden city . . . a disagreeable summer rain was pelting down when we finally straggled into Berlin late in the afternoon. The Russians had not allowed us to look over our sector before coming in although that had been in the agreement and none of us know exactly where to go . . . hundreds of officers and men milled around looked for places to stay in the ruins and most of them wound up sleeping in the rain.'

On 4th July, when a brief ceremony marked the transfer of authority in the Western sectors from the Russians to the Americans, Zhukov again tried to throw a spanner in the works. He said that since Berlin was to be governed by the *Kommandatura* mentioned in the early meetings, and since the *Kommandatura* had not yet been established, the American Sector could not be turned over to the US

The American delegation at the first meeting of the Allied Control Council: General McNarney, presiding, centre; General Clay on his right

forces. The Americans refused to be browbeaten, went into their sector overnight, took over the main administrative buildings and raised the American flag in them. In the morning the Russians were confronted with a *fait accompli* and retired. The first lesson had been learned in how to obtain Russian consent.

Next Zhukov refused to supply the Western sectors with food. Since there was indeed a food shortage in the countryside surrounding Berlin, the Americans and the British accepted this and also accepted the responsibility of supplying food to their own sectors. It was also decided to establish the *Kommandatura* on 10th July.

It is interesting to speculate upon what would have happened had the Russians not insisted on abandoning their responsibility to supply food to non-Russian sectors – or had the West refused to accept. There would not have been total dependence of the Western sectors on the Western Allies; no facilities would have been established for flying food in and the blockade, when it came, would have been that much more disastrous for the inhabitants and, in the absence of a close feeling of mutual trust and co-operation, West Berlin might have fallen an easy prey to the Russians in 1948.

On 11th July came the first meeting of the *Kommandatura* and the Russian's intransigence this time worked to their advantage. They insisted that all orders previously issued by them would remain in effect until further notice. The other three agreed. This was a serious mistake, for all decisions of the *Kommandatura* had to be unanimous. As the Western Allies later came to realise, it was now technically impossible for

Otto Grotewohl

officials established in office by the Soviets immediately after the war to be removed. As Colonel Howley said later: 'When we signed that document we acquiesced to Russian control of Berlin'. The ground work had been laid for the split in the city that was to develop three years later.

Despite all this, the West was still eager to get along with the Russians at almost any price. In Clay 's words: 'Our Government has accepted the principal of our power control and we had determined . . . to create the mutual understanding that would make it successful'. Although it was known that many in the Western sector Government and police still received their orders from East Berlin, in the interest of continued co-operation these ties were not exposed. Four-power Government of Berlin thus continued smoothly for some six months.

In November 1945 the Russians even agreed to a written accord on the air corridors into Berlin. This was of enormous significance to the airlift three years later. Negotiated under American insistence as a result of the need to regularize the heavy air traffic into Berlin, it was in fact the only written accord ever agreed with the Soviet Union in which the right of Allied access was precisely defined.

The first major crisis occurred in early 1946, when the Russians were shown in no uncertain fashion that they could never hope to control the city except by some dramatic new step. They proposed to join the Communist Party and the Social Democratic Party, hoping to capitalize on the fact that Berlin had, since the late 19th century, been a stronghold of socialism. At first it looked as if they might succeed. American and British military officials were apathetic and most Berliners were far too busy fighting hunger and cold in the first post-war winter to be concerned with political

manoeuvre. Moreover the merger had powerful support in the figure of Otto Grotewohl, then Chairman of the SPD in Berlin, and later to be Prime Minister of East Germany. Opposition emerged finally from the socialists themselves. Rebellious delegates overrode Grotewohl and insisted that the merger could not take place without the approval of the entire membership of the party in a special election. Eighty-two per cent of the supposedly extreme left wing Social Democrats in the Western sectors of Berlin voted against such

an amalgamation. In the East, the Russians closed the polls before any results could appear, and announced that in their sector the merger would take place anyway. Thus was created the Social Unity Party, the name of the ruling party in present day East Germany.

Next, in October 1946, on the over-riding authority of the Allied Control Council which governed all Germany, there were to be elections in Berlin to replace the Russian city administration set up at the end of the war. The Russians inaugurated a frantic

pre-election campaign to influence Berliners. Mammoth posters proclaimed: 'The Soviet Union is the friend of the German working people' and: 'New Germany marches to Peace with her Soviet Brothers'. Fresh fruits and vegetables flowed in from the Eastern Sector.

Despite the most energetic efforts, however, on 20th October 1946, with a ninety per cent turnout, the communists were resoundingly defeated. Even in the communist-controlled Eastern Sector of the city the Social Unity Party polled only twenty-one

Results of the first elections since 1932 are published

per cent of the vote, a smaller share that the communists had drawn in Berlin before Hitler came to power.

Thereafter communist political opposition to the Western Allies intensified.

In one particular case Soviet pressure backfired badly. In an attempt to avoid difficulties, the Lord Mayor, Dr Otto Ostrowski, so compromised himself with the Soviets that an outraged City Assembly

35

Left: Social Unity Party election poster. *Above left:* Otto Ostrowski. *Above right:* Ernst Reuter. *Below:* President Truman with Secretary of State George Marshall

threw him out. He was replaced by a leading anti-communist, Ernst Reuter, a key figure in the events of the next two years. Reuter had in fact once been a member of the Communist Party but left it after the First World War. He had opposed Hitler and spent the Nazi years in enforced exile in Turkey, teaching Politics and Economics. When he returned in 1946 he had become one of Berlin's leading Social Democrats. The Soviets, who had never forgiven him for his betrayal, vetoed his election and for eighteen months Reuter was in the strange position of being the duly elected Lord Mayor, but barred from taking office.

During the rest of 1946 it became evident that the Soviet Union did not intend to co-operate in the joint Government of Germany. Repeated Soviet vetoes reduced both the *Kommandatura* and the Allied Control Council to virtual impotence.

By early 1947 the main line of Soviet foreign policy, not only in Berlin but everywhere in Europe, had become apparent. Poland, Rumania and Bulgaria already had Russian style governments, Hungary was soon to fall completely into the Soviet orbit. In Greece the Russians were promoting civil war.

As a result, America reversed her policy of co-operation. Truman, who had followed Roosevelt's policy until it was quite obviously bankrupt, announced what was to become known as the 'Truman Doctrine' of opposition to the spread of communism. That was in March 1947. In June, the Secretary of State, George C Marshall, announced the beginning of the programme of large scale American Economic assistance to promote European recovery in East and West Europe alike. Stalin forbade the Eastern bloc countries from accepting. The ideological battle between the two utterly contrary world outlooks, the American and the Russian, had been joined and Berlin was soon to become the focus for this confronta-

tion. As General Clay said, 'We were now engaged in a competitive struggle, not with arms but with resources, with ideas and ideals . . . there could be no escaping from this struggle . . . we knew not how long it would last or what turn it would take'.

As far as Berlin was concerned, it didn't take them long to find out. Russian propaganda and terrorism reached a new level. In the Soviet zone, Western newspapers, periodicals and books were seized and burned.

The claim was persistently made that all Berlin should be ruled by the communists, since it was within the Soviet controlled sphere of Germany. There were hundreds of little incidents designed to reinforce this by insinuation and outright terror. The Soviets denied the validity of the new City Assembly which was based at City Hall in the Eastern Sector. Letters to the Lord Mayor were returned by the Russians with the explanation that there was no such individual. Four judges whose decisions displeased the Soviets were kidnapped. Kidnappings, indeed, were popular with the communist authorities and easy to arrange. Victims could be picked up in the street and whisked over into the Russian Sector without fear of future investigation.

It was a test of power that was startlingly arbitrary at this early stage. Sometimes an officer would close a bridge with a statement that repairs were needed, yet within an hour he would declare it open again, there never having been any sign of workmen. Sometimes cars were stopped on their way from Berlin and the drivers told they had an incorrect pass, yet the next day the same officer might wave the same cars smilingly through. It should have been clear that things were heading towards a show-down.

Outside Berlin events indicated that this was so. In February 1948, Czechoslovakia fell to the communists and shortly afterwards General Clay assessed the new atmosphere that he

detected: 'For many months . . . I have held that war was unlikely for at least two years. Within the last few weeks I have felt a subtle change in Soviet attitude which I cannot define : . . . other than to describe it as a feeling of new tenseness in every Soviet individual with whom we have official relations'.

Clay's assessment caused intense concern in Washington. He was not a man to be ignored. Although his feelings were not supported by intelligence reports, which continued to contain nothing to arouse suspicion, he was about to become Commander-in-Chief of US Forces in Germany. Until now political considerations had been far from his experience. He had spent most of the war in Washington, had little knowledge of Germany and had conscientiously followed the policies laid down for him. But actions in Germany to date had revealed him as a highly adaptable politician. He had seen the need for Germany to recover industrially and

Marshal Sokolovsky (with cigarette) at an Allied Control Council meeting

had advocated American Economic assistance. He had begun to quetions Soviet motives and, most important of all, he had proved that determined action could get results from the Russians. For all these reasons he remained a beacon of light in the darkness that was about to descend on Berlin.

The campaign intensified when, in March 1948, the Russian member in the Allied Control Council, Marshal Sokolovsky, castigated the Western powers as 'intolerant of genuine democracy', and in the next meeting, on 20th March, stalked out of the conference room, followed by the entire Soviet delegation. The four-party administration of Germany had collapsed. Several strategists foresaw the imminence of three crises, each worse than the previous one. Berlin, isolated within the Communist Sector, could fall – that was the first

The Press interviews the MP escorts of an Allied train which was halted at the border and returned to its destination

possibility. Secondly, although the Western Allies were committed to German reunification it was now clear that reunification could only occur on communist terms. Thirdly, if that happened the border of Russia's empire would advance to the Rhine and all Europe would be threatened by a communist takeover as never before.

Clay was soon given an opportunity to test the steadfastness of his resolve. On 1st April the Russians announced that they would check all baggage and freight shipments and all passengers on military trains. If the Americans refused, the trains would be halted at the border. This was a clear contradiction to the free and unrestricted right of access to Berlin, a condition under which the Western Allies had evacuated the Eastern Zone.

Apprehensively the Department of the Army in Washington asked Clay whether American dependents should

be flown out of Berlin. 'Never', he replied, 'it would be politically disastrous. Withdrawal of dependents from Berlin would create hysteria accompanied by a rush of Germans to communism for safety. The conditions would spread in Europe and would increase communist political strength everywhere'. Summing up the situation in the simplest terms, he said: 'when Berlin falls, West Germany will be next. If we mean to hold Europe against communism we must not budge.'

As good as his word, Clay sent in a

A Russian officer is refused entry into a building in the American zone

test train with an armed guard detachment. It was, as the Russians had promised, shunted into a siding and eventually had to be withdrawn ignominiously.

There was nothing for it, at least in Clay's determined view, but to supply the American forces in Berlin by a small airlift, and this began at once. Soviet pressure increased correspondingly. The East Berlin police force was incorporated into that of

A truck equipped with PA loudspeakers relays news during the power cuts

the Soviet Zone, barge traffic between West Berlin and the West was restricted and in May all freight shipments were required to have additional documentation. The climax came in June. On the 10th, after an abortive attempt to remove trains and rolling stock from the American Sector, the Russians temporarily suspended rail traffic between Berlin and West Germany. Two days later it was just as suddenly restored. Also, on 12th June, the Soviets closed the Berlin-Helmstedt Autobahn to repair the Elbe river bridge. On 16th June the Russians walked out of the *Kommandatura*. There was now no longer any semblance of four-power unity.

The final confrontation came over an economic question: currency reform. All Berlin had been in a state of total confusion for months over the

rampant inflation that had hit the city. This was the result of the Russians having a duplicate set of plates with which to print Occupation Marks. These plates had been given to the Russians in 1945 and as a result they were free to print an unlimited number of notes, more than were redeemable at face value from the United States treasury.

On 18th June the Western occupation authorities announced that a new West Mark would be introduced. In retaliation, four days later, on 23rd June, the Soviets announced a new East Mark and proclaimed it as the only legal tender for East Germany and all of Berlin. Meanwhile the Western authorities had moved ahead to incorporate West Berlin's currency with that of West Germany. In a cloak and dagger operation of the strictest secrecy, they flew in 250 million new West Marks in cases marked 'Whisky', 'Gin' and 'Brandy'. On 23rd June, the same day the

Russians announced their currency reform, the cases were broken open and on the next day the announcement was made that West Berlin had a new currency.

One of the results of the rival currency orders was that the Soviet occupation authorities in Berlin had a splendid pretext to intimidate the City Government. When it convened on the afternoon of 23rd June, to pass the reforms, the way to the City Hall was blocked by thousands of communist demonstrators, many of whom even entered the building and took over the Chamber and the Gallery. When the meeting finally began, the Assembly, in a courageous demonstration, threw out Marshal Sokolovsky's currency order and said that it would apply only to the Soviet Sector. Afterwards the democratic members were set upon by communist thugs and the Eastern Sector police refused to intervene. One policeman who escorted several delegates to safety was discharged the following day.

This was the excuse the Soviets had been waiting for. At 6 am on 24th June 1948, all traffic to and from Berlin was severed.

The Eastern Sector teleprinters in the offices of West Berlin newspapers clattered out: 'The transport division of the Soviet military administration is compelled to halt all passengers and freight traffic from Berlin tomorrow at 0600 hours because of technical difficulties. Water traffic will be suspended, coal shipments from the Soviet Zone are halted'. The Soviet authorities also announced that West Berlin would receive electricity only between 11.00pm and 1.00am. What General Clay described as 'One of the most ruthless efforts in modern times to use mass starvation for political coercion', had begun.

A bridge in the sky

For a day the fate of the city and perhaps the fate of Europe hung in the balance. In Berlin itself a minor crisis threatened when a Soviet radio bulletin announced that the water supply in West Berlin was about to fail. West Berlin housewives rushed to hoard water and were on the verge of really causing a breakdown when the American radio in a calculated gamble announced, 'Give your baby a bath; plenty of water is available'. Once the Berliners were reassured the demand subsided.

There still remained the problem of what was to be done, and the decision was taken by the one man who kept absolutely firm during the crisis, Lieutenant-General Lucius Clay himself. Everyone else was uncertain, his own officers were divided and some even wanted to withdraw completely: 'If your hand is in the fire,' said one, 'why not pull it out?' No advice was forthcoming from Washington. Clay was on his own.

A few hours after the blockade was declared, Clay was sitting late over supper with a Lieutenant-General Albert Wedemeyer who was chief of the Planning and Operations Division of the US General Staff. 'Why not,' suggested Wedemeyer, 'consider supplying the city by air?' He was, perhaps, the only man in Germany at the time who could have made such a suggestion seriously, for he had served during the war with United States forces in China where his men and the Chinese troops had, for three years, been supplied principally by planes flying over the Himalayas – The Hump – from India. For those three years, up to 72,000 tons a month of food, oil, ammunition, medical supplies, mules and machinery had been airlifted to the American and Chinese forces. It had been the biggest airlift in the world at the time but the suppliers had the advantage that the airlift did not have to be continuous and they had a wide choice of landing areas.

Berlin would need twice the Hump tonnage – over 140,000 per month; it would have to be continuous through all weathers; and it would be limited to three twenty-mile wide corridors and two landing fields in Berlin.

Clay called up Ernst Reuter, the debarred Lord Mayor of Berlin. If Berlin were supplied by air could his people last out during the winter? Reuter came back with the essential toughness of spirit that Clay was looking for. According to Willy

C54 'Skymaster' during the air lift

45

General Wedemeyer

General Lemay

Brandt, himself later to be Mayor of Berlin and, as now, Federal Chancellor of West Germany, Reuter said: 'We shall, in any case, continue on our way; do what you are able to do, we shall do what we feel to be our duty'. The Berliners, he said, were prepared to fight for their liberties.

The next morning General Clay called General Curtis LeMay, Chief of the United States Air Force in Europe, and asked him if his planes could perform what he said was 'a very big operation'. Could they supply 5–700 tons a day to Berlin? (Clay saw it at this time purely as a short term measure to gain time for negotiations with the Russians.)

There were very few planes around with which to start such an operation. Of the 12,000 American planes that had darkened the skies over Europe three years previously, most had long since flown home to be lined up in rows in Arizona waiting to be broken up. All the Americans had were eighty C-47s, affectionately known as Gooney Birds. They were troop carrying versions of the old DC3 passenger plane of the 1930s and they were not much use as freighters: they could carry about three tons each at a speed of 170mph.

But they were better than nothing, and the next day – 25th June – thirty-two flights left the American Rhein-Maine Air Force base near Frankfurt and landed some eighty tons of supplies in Berlin, mostly milk for children, flour and medicine.

On 26th June the wavering administration in Washington rallied to support Clay's decision. Response was slow, certainly – there had been no proper warning from the CIA that a crisis was imminent and there was no policy decided on how to deal with it – but Truman's response when it came was everything Clay could have asked for. By his personal order every available plane in the European command was pressed into service for

US air base, Rhein-Main airport

the airlift, and when asked at a White House meeting about American policy in Berlin the President said simply, 'The United States is going to stay. Period.'

On 30th June the British House of Commons, in the person of Foreign Secretary Ernest Bevin, announced a similar determination. He said that the decision to remain in Berlin could lead to a grave situation but, 'None of us can accept surrender . . . we cannot abandon those stout-hearted Berlin democrats who are refusing to bow to Soviet pressure'.

If the political leaders were certain, however, they did not carry the rest of their administrations with them. Both the Department of Defense in Washington and the army considered the Allied position in the isolated city militarily unsound. The air staff in the Pentagon refused for almost a month to increase the number of transport planes in Europe. They said that so great a concentration of aircraft would be militarily unwise, and that it was not worthwhile risking war over Berlin. In the end, in mid-July, President Truman overruled them.

Ernest Bevin

Clay, Reuter, Truman: these three together had taken the decision to stay in Berlin while the people of Berlin themselves and the top rank administrators wavered. In the circumstances even the slightest hint of indecision by the West could have allowed the councils of those seeking their peace with the East to prevail.

All of Berlin was soon convinced, however, that the Western Allies were there to stay. Reuter and the local SPD chairman, Franz Neumann, held a meeting on the day the blockade was announced. Neumann compared the communists with Hitler and announced forthrightly that 'Berlin will remain free; it will never become communist', and closed the meeting with an appeal to the world to come

The first flights bring supplies for children

Franz Neumann

49

British control tower at Gatow

to Berlin's assistance. Almost from the start of the airlift, on 25th June, most Berliners were convinced that they would not be abandoned.

The British too got an airlift operation under way, as of 30th June. They used DC3s and at first called their operation 'Carter Paterson', later changing its name, rather wittily, to 'Plane fare'. (It was altered because the Russians pointed out that Carter Paterson was the name of a famous removals firm and insisted that the operation was intended to remove troops from Berlin, rather than support the Allied presence.)

In the early days both operations were separate, the British using the northern corridor to approach Berlin flying from Wunstorf, near Hanover, to Gatow, and the Americans the southern. Both departed by the centre corridor.

Berlin's major airport, Tempelhof, was utterly unsuited to take the vast amount of traffic. It had hardly been improved since the 1930s when it had just one grass runway. Now the Americans had built another runway, a base of rubble topped with metal landing strips. Planes landed on the metal and took off on the grass. The approach to it was hair-raising since it was closely surrounded by enormous blocks of flats and one end was dominated by a 400 foot chimney stack belonging to a brewer who steadfastly refused to knock it down.

The men, too, were ill-prepared. None of the pilots had had experience in air-freighting and General Curtis LeMay was best known for his bombing experience. (It was he who had supervised the dropping of the atomic bombs on Hiroshima and Nagasaki, which scarcely had any relevance to delivering supplies to a besieged city.) The 160 pilots were driven to the limit, having only three or four hours sleep a night and working seven days a week, yet morale was high and the complaints were not of a serious nature. Indeed, the most widely reported incident was something of light relief. The crew of a Gooney Bird flying in supplies for the French occupation forces discovered that part of their cargo consisted of wine.

They refused to take it in. It's priority they said, was hardly that of milk for starving children; and why should the French have wine when the Americans did not even have Coca-Cola? The French were outraged and dispatched a delegation to the US Air Force headquarters with a dietary history of France to prove that wine was absolutely vital to their constitution. They had their way.

Gradually the operation got into its stride. On the fourth day 384 tons were lifted in and by mid-July Berlin was receiving 1,500 tons of supplies a day by air.

There was still a long way to go. Berlin normally imported 15,000 tons a day, but it was estimated that the city could get along on just over a quarter of this – 4,500 tons – if requirements were reduced to the bare essentials.

Much of the burden was now being borne by four-engine C-54s, military versions of the DC4s, which could carry almost ten tons at a cruising speed of 180mph. Within a few weeks there were to be 225 of these machines on the job backed up by another hundred being used to ferry supplies from the States.

As soon as the C54s arrived at Rhein-Main, they were stripped of their long range navigational equipment, their extra fuel tanks, partitions, troop benches, wash stands and everything else that could be removed. In their place went flour, cheese, vegetables and meat, and within a few hours of the time of their arrival they were flying to Berlin in their new role.

The British too stepped up their activity with four-engined Yorks, Dakotas, and a few Sunderland flying boats. These had a special use – their hulls were protected against corrosive salt water and they were used to carry all the salt into the city. They landed on a lake in the British Sector of the city and were unloaded by small boats.

Improvisation was the key to this early part of the operation. At Gatow

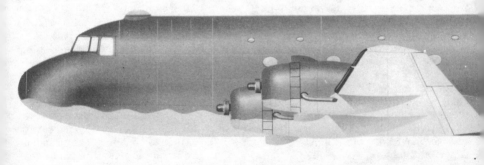

Loading wheat into a C54

The US Douglas C-54 Skymaster transport and cargo carrier. Developed from the pre-war triple-tailed DC-4 airliner, which was too big to meet US airlines' requirements, the C-54 was slightly smaller than its predecessor, and first flew in April 1942. *Engines*: Four Pratt & Whitney R-2000 radials, 1,350hp each. *Accommodation*: Up to 42 passengers. *Speed*: 265mph. *Climb*: 1,350 feet per minute. *Ceiling*: 26,600 feet. *Range*: 3,800 miles maximum. *Weight empty/loaded*: 36,980/73,000lbs. *Span*: 117 feet 6 inches. *Length*: 93 feet 11 inches

The Douglas C-74 Globemaster was an advanced development of the C-54 Skymaster transport, but was built in very limited numbers only. *Engines:* four Pratt & Whitney R-4360 Wasp Major radials, 3,500-hp each. *Cruising speed:* 193 mph. *Gross weight:* 165,000 lbs. *Payload:* 55,586 lbs. *Span:* 173 feet 3 inches. *Length:* 124 feet 2 inches.

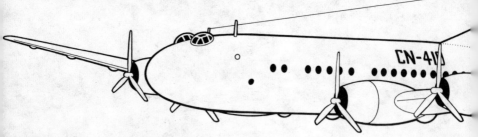

The Avro York was a transport version of the same company's Lancaster bomber, making use of its predecessor's wings, engines, undercarriage, and empennage, with the addition of an extra, central fin. *Engines:* four Rolls-Royce Merlin inlines, 1,280-hp each. *Speed:* 210 mph cruise at 10,000 feet. *Weight empty/loaded:* 45,000/ 70,000 lbs. *Payload:* 10,000 lbs. *Span:* 102 feet. *Length:* 78 feet 6 inches.

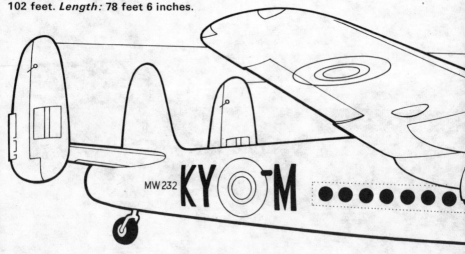

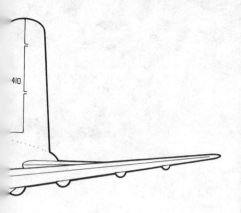

A Volkswagen for Berlin's police is loaded aboard a York at Wunstorf

Sunderland flying boats in the British
sector

The Short Sunderland Mark V was the final development version of this famous
World War II reconnaissance/bomber flying boat, and proved useful during the
Berlin airlift as it could operate from the lakes in the area without disturbing
conventional travel from airfields and airports. *Engines:* four Pratt & Whitney
R-1830 Twin Wasp radials, 1,200-hp each at takeoff. *Speed:* 213 mph at 5,000 feet.
Ceiling: 17,900 feet. *Range:* 2,980 miles. *Weight empty/loaded:* 37,000/60,000 lbs.
Payload: about 7,000 lbs. *Span:* 112 feet 9½ inches. *Length:* 85 feet 4 inches.

the metal runway soon started to break up with the constant hammering of heavily laden aircraft. At first, there was no surfacing and no equipment for repairs. Soon, someone pointed out that there was at least a ready source of bitumen – the broken road surfaces in the bombed out areas of the city. To process it, the RAF Work Services assembled in the corner of the airfield an extraordinary conglomeration of obsolete boilers which were promptly nicknamed 'Dante's Inferno'. Rapidly they collected crushers, dumpers and a First World War vintage steam roller to flatten out the odd mixture that they produced. Within a few days they had even acquired a modern steam roller. An East German driver from Leipzig had trundled his machine through miles of Russian controlled country-side simply in order to offer his services. No one could understand

Women maintain Tempelhof airfield

how he had managed to pass through the check points on the route.

Tempelhof had a similar make-shift arrangement. A labour force of 220 German civilians stood by with shovels and wheelbarrows loaded with asphalt and sand at the edges of the runway. As soon as a plane landed they hurried on to the strip to repair the damage, scrambling off three minutes later to avoid being hit by the next plane. In this way they could keep the metal runway in some sort of repair while engineers laid out additional hard surfaces.

Things got much worse when the Yorks started flying. They landed at Wunstorf on 1st July 1948. None of the ten crews knew what they were undertaking, merely thinking that the job had grown too big for the little Dakotas to handle. Catastrophe struck at once. The day after their arrival it began to rain and it rained solidly for eighteen hours. Twenty-six Dakotas were put out of action by electrical troubles and the aircraft which did not have hard-standings – the parking spaces were reserved for the Dakotas – bogged down while the loading trucks, which continually ran to and fro across the airfield, churned the light soil into a mass of mud almost a foot deep.

To taxi out of the mud all four engines of the Yorks had to be set at half power, and immediately the pilot hit the perimeter track he had to shut down the throttles and clamp on the brakes or else the great planes would plunge across the track and come to rest in the mud on the other side.

Even when the weather turned warmer and the mud dried, conditions did not improve very much. The mud turned into hard ridges of packed, dried earth and bulldozers had to be called in to level it off. After that,

Above: Ruhr coal is flown to Berlin. *Below:* Rewards in the form of cigarettes were given to crews to increase their loading speed. *Below right:* Newly installed landing lights at Tempelhof

every time an engine started, a gigantic cloud of dust flew across the airfield. The dust caused its own problems: it settled on the windscreens of the planes and when these flew into clouds the dust turned into mud and ran messily down to obscure the pilot's vision. When the windscreen wipers were switched on to clear the mess, gritty particles scratched the plastic screens and landing flares turned the scratches into blinding curves of light.

The arrival of the Yorks turned organisation into a nightmare. The mess was full whenever it was open and flight schedules were at first chaotic; for a time aircraft were making their final approaches straight down an air corridor as other aircraft took off towards them. Under this sort of pressure, it was clear that Wunstorf alone would not be adequate to handle the traffic needed to run the British side of the airlift. It was decided that the Dakota aircraft should move to Fassberg, a disused airfield some forty miles to the North. It was a good choice: there

were twelve large hangars, a spur from the local railway served the airfield and it was well surfaced. Within a week it was ready to undertake its new task and on 19th July the Dakotas began the revolutionary ordeal of flying Ruhr coal to Berlin.

In July, the first full month of the Berlin airlift, anyone looking for excitement would be more likely to find it on the ground. The twenty-seven reported incidents however, were minute. Loading lorries dented the edges of wings, cranes scraped fuselages, pilots knocked their machines against hangers. An instrument repairer stood on a loaded Verey-pistol and started a fire. One pilot had to jettison his load of hay when the port engine of his Dakota began belching white smoke, but he made it back to Wunstorf in safety. Other planes developed fuel leaks, electrical faults, exhaust failures – all in all nothing very dramatic.

Rewards in the form of cigarettes were doled to handling crews to increase their loading and unloading speeds. Perhaps the record was

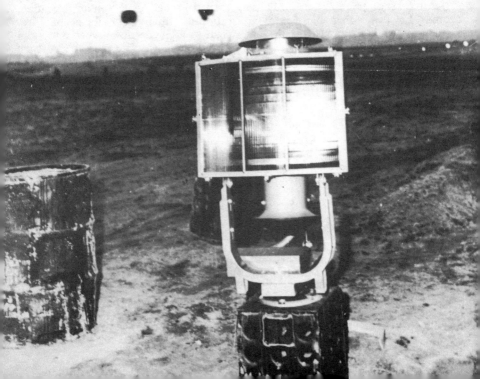

established by twelve labourers at Rhein-Main who loaded a C-54 with nine tons of coal in five minutes and forty-five seconds, for which they received a whole pack of cigarettes each.

Most of the problems indeed were ground problems. All the spare parts had been used up within a fortnight and had to be imported from the States. Railway timetables had to be devised to provide supplies to the airbases, approach roads had to be remetalled, airport lighting had to be rebuilt.

These were aspects, however, that were largely ignored by the press who were filing frantic tales of derring-do to the newspapers of the world. It was certainly dramatic to see planes leaving Tempelhof every three minutes – a landing or a takeoff every ninety seconds. But in fact once in the air the dangers were considerably less. The planes were staggered in three different levels 500 feet apart, which meant that the plane in front at any one of these elevations was twenty miles ahead.

Despite the paucity of mid-air dramas however, correspondents insisted on sending back stories such as the following:

'We start to roll, Gerry isn't sitting back relaxed, the skin is tight on the back of his neck, the plane gathers momentum slowly, it creeps and groans with the effort, we are half way down the runway now and the plane feels as soggy as a sackful of wet wheat. Slowly, agonisingly, the plane climbs and then after some five minutes Gerry raises his head and sits back.'

Such tension was largely artificial; pilots had been flying this way in commercial airlines for about fourteen years. The worst thing that the aircrews suffered was plain fatigue: after some weeks of the airlift, 391 crew members were questioned about conditions and some 170 complained of lack of sleep. Serious, perhaps, over the long term, but scarcely dramatic.

There were always those, of course, ready to enliven the boredom with a bit of wit. Many Americans used to give their positions in rhyme, 'I'm a Yankee with a blackened soul, bound for Gatow with a load of coal.' There was an Irishman named B T O'Reilly who enriched the wavelengths from his cockpit of his Lancaster with tunes on a mouth organ, and another Lancaster pilot, whose plane registration letters ended in TB·never called them before announcing his position – he just gave a gasping tuberculoid cough.

Some reports stressed the menace of the Russians. This was another potential danger which never developed. No Russian aircraft ever challenged the airlift planes, probably because this was the only means of access that was covered by a formal written agreement.

The most important thing on the flight to Berlin was that the pilot should exactly follow the prescribed flying procedure: to the Darmstadt radio beacon at 3,000 feet, an exact turn to the Aschaffenburg beacon, climbing until he reached his prescribed altitude of between 5,000 and 6,500 feet, a thirty-three degree turn at Aschaffenburg to reach the Fulda beacon forty-five miles away, listening in there to the pilot in front of him to check that he was exactly three minutes behind. Forty minutes later the pilot would switch into Tempelhof, swing over the Wedding beacon, turn right, circle over the broken city towards a large apartment building, leave the 400-foot chimney away to his left, land, and follow the yellow jeep which whipped in front of him bearing the sign 'Follow Me'.

A few weeks after the start of the airlift the American and British operations combined, and on 22nd August American planes began to fly from the British base at Fassberg.

The arrival of the big C54s at Fassberg dramatised the difference between the American and the British contributions to the airlift. The British, having been at war earlier than the Americans, had concentrated on building bombers, whereas the Americans, with a greater demand for peacetime aircraft, had developed larger transport planes. The American C54 had been designed as a transport aircraft to carry heavy loads, whereas the York, its nearest British equivalent in type and numbers, was a comparatively small-scaled development of a bomber.

There were differences in operation as well: the British were used to flying in formation and with their radar aids could tell within ten seconds when they would arrive over any given beacon. The American force, doing its navigation by time and distance, was not nearly as accurate. Frequently a C54 would have to circle a beacon to lose time or increase speed considerably in order to make up time on the other side. As a result, American aircrews were squeamish about the limits of separation imposed by the British at Fassberg: two minutes and 500 feet were not enough for them. They did not appreciate that British pilots, for the most part former bomber men, had been used to operating in forces of 750 to 1,000 aircraft on night raids, without lights, taking off from congested areas. The chances of collision then had seemed so much greater that the airlift corridor operations seemed relatively easy.

This did not, however, make up for the greater carrying capacity and the efficiency of the C54s. Fassberg's American era opened with five squadrons, one from Japan, one from Honolulu, one from Texas, one from Alaska and one which was already based in Europe. They came in at short notice. The Alaskan crews arrived still wearing their Parkas and other Arctic equipment, while the crews from Honolulu were in lightweight summer kit.

The new arrivals strained Anglo-American relations to the limit, especially over one surprising question: the cinema. Showing what films when was easily decided – three British and three American films a week, with a German variety show on the seventh night, but putting this policy into practice was something else again. The American Motion Picture Corporation, which catered for the American forces, laid down that a GI or an officer paid a fixed price for his seat and could sit anywhere. But the British Army Kinema Corporation set up three prices. GIs soon became baffled and annoyed. On one day of the week a GI could walk up to the box office, put down twenty cents, go in and sit where he liked, but the next day when he put down his twenty cents he would be asked which of three seats he wanted – in British currency – and when he had worked that one out he would then be ushered to a seat which, on a basis of free choice, he might well have avoided. The next night everything would be back to 'normal' again. Multiply this by 4,000 – the number of GIs in Fassberg – and the strain on Anglo-American relations becomes apparent.

None of this, however, affected the metronome regularity of the flights. Clay was so confident that the Russians would attempt no drastic measures and so certain that the airlift had demonstrated Western determination that he suggested calling their bluff by running the blockade with an armoured convoy down the autobahn to Berlin. 'I feel that the world is now facing the most vital issue that has developed since Hitler', he said, 'only we have the strength to halt this aggressive policy here and now . . . I am sure that determined action will bring it to a halt now without war. It can be stopped only if we assume some risk.' He was probably right; the Russians would not have fought for Berlin. But his dramatic suggestion was never put to the test.

The Douglas C-47 Skytrain, military counterpart of the celebrated DC-3 airliner, served with nearly every Allied air force and in every theatre in World War II, carrying more cargo than all the other types of transport aircraft put together. With their easily-loaded fuselages crammed with essential supplies, they formed the backbone of the Allied airlift into Berlin.

Engines: two Pratt & Whitney R-1830 Twin Wasp radials, 1,200-hp each at takeoff. *Speed:* 230 mph. *Ceiling:* 23,200 feet. *Range:* 2,125 miles. *Weight empty/loaded:* 16,865/31,000 lbs. *Payload:* 9,450 lbs. *Span:* 95 feet. *Length:* 64 feet 6 inches.

C-47 Dakotas

The testing time

The first month of the airlift, when there were still food supplies available, was a time of total confusion for the Berliners. When forced to confront their situation by public opinion surveys, only a third of the population thought that the airlift would be successful, the remainder expected that there would be a war or that the Russians would simply walk in and the Allies depart.

In fact few of them thought about the problem at all; most knew there were reserves of food for the immediate future and that was enough. They were totally taken up with the problems of day to day living. The generating equipment that the Russians had ripped out had never been replaced, the limited generating capacity that was left ran street transport during the day and allowed very limited current for industrial use. Households could never rely on more than a few hours' supply at a time. From the Eastern Sector the Russians made what play they could with the situation, newspapers and the radio prophesying imminent starvation, death, plague and water shortage.

Western and Eastern sectors banned each other's money and no-one knew how much any of the Marks were worth or their relationship one to

A favourite occupation: Berliners watch the arrival of another vital consignment

another. No wonder the people were more concerned with the harsh realities of their day to day life than with the political implications of the airlift. One Berliner, an architect, was quoted as saying: 'In the West we must be against the Russians and in the East against the Americans – wherever you happen to be that's the only way to prove yourself a true democrat, so I say that there is nothing for us Germans to do but be neutral and wait until Stalin and Truman finish playing their own little game'.

Besides, in the early days the Berliners themselves had as much reason to blame the Western Allies as be thankful to them. The way the incoming supplies were earmarked, one ton fed fifty of the foreign occupation troops, but 500 Berliners; many unscrupulous Americans and British battened on the hapless population,

buying pianos, silver and china from destitute Berlin families for derisory sums; the foreigners had their clubs where they ate steaks and drank wine and spirits; they could hire Germans, often college graduates, for a pound or two a week.

The resentment this caused, however, was rapidly dissipated by the airlift. Berliners were soon studying the daily tonnage reports in the newspapers, watching the planes land at Tempelhof as a favourite recreation. Airmen received gifts, many pilots wearing small amulets knitted by German children. When a C-47 crashed early in the airlift there was an enormous flood of sympathy for the families of the two airmen who died in it. A nameless Berliner placed a plaque at the sight of the crash. 'You gave your lives for us,' read the inscription, 'the Berliners of the West sectors will never forget you'.

But the airlift as yet made life no more than just possible. The planes brought in dehydrated vegetables and salted meat, but for practically everything else the Berliners learned to make do as best they could. Since there were as yet no restrictions on travel, the underground stations were daily crowded with people carrying satchels, sacks and boxes as they went to the Eastern Sector in search of cabbages, lettuces, cauliflowers and turnips. Others bicycled or walked pulling little wheeled carts behind them. Gardens were cultivated as never before. People laboriously excavated tree stumps which they could burn. There were no new clothes at all and most children went barefoot. There was no glass to mend broken windows, no private transport except bicycles, no spare parts, no malt for beer, no typewriter ribbons for offices, no paint, no cosmetics, no hardware, no toys.

All these afflictions gave the Russians opportunity, as they

An outdoor memorial service for two US pilots who died during the air lift

Daily trips to the Eastern sector in search of food

thought, for engineering political advantage. In the middle of July they issued a dramatic decree that all Berlin would henceforth be fed by themselves. The communist press announced, 'Airlift has no purpose – in future all Berliners can buy their rations in the Eastern Sector'. There was one trifling requirement laid on the Western population: it must register in the East, then its members could buy all the food they needed.

To the disgust of the communists this offer was largely ignored. Only 85,000 people – a mere 3·2 per cent of the more than two and a half million strong Western population – took advantage of it.

Surprisingly, the man who was ostensibly responsible for putting Russian policy into effect – Marshal Vasily Sokolovsky – was quite popular as a person. He was mild, well-mannered and his greatest fault was collaring anyone who he could interest to show them pictures of his two children. He made a point of divorcing his social life from his official life and one Western official who knew him said of him: 'He is a man who you would like to have as your friend, and he would be a credit to any country'. Once, after he was stopped by American traffic control for speeding in his black limousine at 65mph in a 20mph zone, General Clay paid a visit to him to apologise for the inconvenience.

Nevertheless the split between the East and West zones widened. In the summer of 1948 the Western sectors acquired their own police. Up to July the police force was still headed by Paul Markgraf, the ex-Nazi officer who had been converted to communism. During that month he began to weed out non-communists from the police force, dismissing nearly 600 of them. At this point the city government suspended him and made a non-communist professional policeman, Johannes Stumm, Acting

71

Johannes Stumm

Police President in his place. The Russians countermanded the order in their sector and Stumm established his own headquarters in the Western Zone, informing the police force that it was up to the individual to decide which of the two police chiefs to obey. From that point on the city had in effect two police forces who were – on several occasions literally – at daggers drawn.

Meanwhile, in the outside world, the split between East and West was rather less clear cut. Neither France nor Britain were convinced that the airlift had yet been proven, and both were prepared to reach a negotiated settlement with Russia. America went along with them. At the beginning of August the three Western ambassadors in Moscow requested a personal interview with Stalin. The

The once neat lawns of the Berlin Zoo are given over to potato growing

73

Communists attempt to break up a
council meeting

British MPs keep angry anti-communist crowds from damaging the Soviet War memorial near the Brandenburg Gate

four of them worked out an agreement: the West would recognise the East Mark as the sole currency in Berlin and the Soviets would lift the blockade. Very significantly, Stalin agreed verbally that when this had been put into effect the West could share control of the new currency. Typically, his words were not, however, incorporated in the written agreement which followed.

When Clay heard of it in Berlin he was at once suspicious. He was sure the Russians would not, when the time came, allow any sharing in the control. When the four military Governors in Berlin were due to take action, Clay insisted that any arrangement was dependent on an agreement in advance of any action over the control of the currency. Marshal Sokolovsky refused to include Stalin's verbal comment and negotiations broke down. By insisting on adhering to Stumm's verbal undertaking, Clay had effectively prevented the possibility of a Russian takeover. Both sides blamed the other for the collapse of the talks and the position was back to square one.

In Berlin itself, the city administration was the next victim of Soviet pressure. Failure to control currency reform and the police led to an increase in Russian harassment.

Truckloads of youthful communists were shipped in to disrupt the meetings of the Assembly in the Eastern Sector, while East German guards stood around idly watching them.

A *Time* magazine correspondent reported an incident which showed how meticulously planned these 'spontaneous' demonstrations really were. During the first major attempt at disruption on 26th August a few youths surged towards an iron gate of the Assembly building. Apparently this was a premature move, for a policeman stepped out in front and shouted in outrage: 'No, no, not now; *first* you finish singing the "Internationale", *then* we let you break down the gate'.

On 6th September the majority of the Assembly's members gave up in despair and moved their headquarters to the British Sector, meeting in the Taverna Academia building. Henceforth this became the West Berlin City Hall. The decision to move had been taken despite the presence in the Assembly building of forty-six Western police. After the administrators had moved out, Red Army troops surrounded the building, besieged the Sector police and eventually carted them off to a Soviet Sector prison.

As a result of this exceptionally high-handed action, on 9th September a protest meeting took place in the Platz der Republik, a huge square flanked by the gutted Reichstag building on one side, and on another by the towering Brandenburg Gate

which marks the boundary between the British and Russian and Russian sectors. Three hundred thousand people blanketed the rubble-strewn area, standing quietly as a Social Democrat leader proclaimed: 'He who surrenders Berlin, surrenders the world, surrenders himself!'

What happened next was spontaneous, unplanned – and very significant. Over a period of two hours many minor incidents took place, expressive of dissatisfaction with and hatred of the Soviets. Stones were tossed at police and Soviet cars were pelted on sight until Soviet reinforcements arrived and fired over and into the crowd – one fifteen-year-old by was hit in the stomach and died. During these occurrences four or five boys climbed to the top of the Brandenburg Gate and tore down the Red Flag. The British military police arrived and positioned themselves between the Russian troops and the crowd, which slowly dispersed. More than ten per cent of the population of West Berlin had gathered that day before the Reichstag, a devastating expression of both their anger at the blockade and confidence in their ability to survive.

Shortly afterwards the Russians gave up their attemps to intimidate the city government, and started the process of incorporating East Berlin into the Soviet Zone. They began by dismissing local non-communist officials and by the end of October 2,000 had been dispensed with. Government departments which had been in what was now the Eastern Sector of the city for some hundred years or more were laboriously shifted to the West, a task which was largely completed by the middle of November. Also in mid-November the Soviets dismissed the chiefs of various city departments and at the end of the month they held what they called 'an extraordinary session of the City

Children evacuated by Sunderland flying boats to West Germany

Assembly', consisting of 15,000 carefully selected communist functionaries at which a mayor and a new city executive body were elected. As a result, Berlin for the first time now had two city governments. The split was almost complete.

These activities were largely due to the new confidence in the West created by the success of the airlift. In the words of one manual worker, 'It gave us the certainty that we were not alone'. Another recalled what it was like when, as occasionally happened, the airlift came to a halt: 'Suddenly there is a paralysing silence, it weighs on one like the silence of a corpse, all at once a whole city is listening to stillness, and in the breasts of hundreds of thousands terrible uncertainty begins to arise – are they going to abandon us? Will we have to submit? Then after an eternity the roar can be heard again and there are a hundred thousand sighs of relief.'

As that summer drew to an end both town and occupation forces prepared for the hard winter to come. The RAF inaugurated Operation Stork to airlift children to safety. 15,000 of them were taken out to a better life in West Germany and many families must have been cheered by letters like this one: 'Every morning I have milk and eggs which I am allowed to get for myself in the hen house. I already know all of the cows and pigs, one of whom is called Lotchen. When I come back you will not know me any more because I am getting so big and strong.'

At the end of July 1948, the US side of the airlift had acquired a new leader. Major General Tunner had been appointed over the heads of General Clay and Smith on a special recommendation from Wedemeyer to General Vandenberg, Chief of Staff of the US Air Force. Clay, LeMay and Smith were naturally angered, as they thought they were doing a pretty good job. In addition Tunner was, in the words of the official historian of

the Air Transport Commander, 'an unusually handsome man, cold in manner . . . somewhat arrogant, brilliant, competent' – not the sort of man to win popularity with his colleagues.

But Wedemeyer knew what he was doing. General Tunner was America's, perhaps the world's leading authority on airlifting. He had originally been the head of Ferrying Command, which was created to deliver tens of thousands of aeroplanes from the US factories in which they were built to combat areas. The job of piloting these planes demanded exactly the opposite qualities to combat flying: care, caution, willingness to endure boredom and routine.

In 1944 he had been assigned to command the Hump airlift from India to China. There, within a year, he tripled the quantity of supplies delivered and cut the accident rate eight-fold. He was sure he could improve the performance of the Berlin airlift and he viewed press stories of sustained excitement, of long hours, of exhausted pilots, of frenzy and flap, very coolly: 'Successful operations are not built on such methods,' he said, 'the actual operation of a successful airlift is about as glamorous as drops of water on a stone. There is no frenzy, no flap, just the inexorable process of getting the job done. The real excitement comes from seeing a dozen lines climbing steadily on a chart – tonnage delivered, utilisation of aircraft and so on – and the lines indicating accidents and injuries going sharply down.' On his arrival he found that his fears were justified. The airlift was in his view a bustling 'cowboy operation'. For the flyers themselves the soul-destroying monotony of routine contrasted with an inefficient semblance of excitement and urgency at either end; then the crews got out of their planes to smoke, lounge and gossip in a snack bar.

A new turn-around procedure was

General William Tunner

arranged after Tunner's first trip. Henceforth every plane was met by two jeeps, one with an operations officer and the other with a weather man to brief the pilot. A third vehicle, a Volkswagen van, was a mobile snack bar staffed by the prettiest *fräulein* available. Dissatisfaction and resentment among the crews dissipated rapidly, and turnaround time was brought down to thirty minutes flat.

Tunner also took corrective action against other features making for low morale. The ex-combat pilots doing the dismal routine work demanded by the airlift were irked by their job and had no real conception of its importance to Berlin, their own country or to the fate of Western Europe. In addition they were temporarily staffed, housed in crowded conditions and found it hard to get rest with the constant coming and going of relief crews. This was particularly resented

Arrivals at a Swiss airport

because the permanent occupation forces engaged in other tasks had comparatively luxurious accommodation (General LeMay, for instance, being quartered in a fifty-five room mansion). No provision had been made for aircrew's wives or families.

Tunner immediately set about restoring morale by giving the men a sense of the importance of what they were doing. He started a newspaper, *The Task Force Times*, which, as well as humourously reporting the disagreeable aspects of airlift flying, listed the tonnages each day and began to instil a spirit of competition in the men who were doing the work.

The new appointee also initiated a series of lengthy staff meetings. These rapidly revealed that the major obstacles in the way of more efficient operations were to be found on the ground. The airlift needed more ground personnel, weathermen, cooks, mechanics, engineers, radio men, radar men, doctors, carpenters and drivers. The bases needed technical improvement in runways, taxiways, hard surfaces, fueling facilities, loading and unloading facilities, hangar space, flood-lighting. There were not enough railways to bring goods to the airbases. Cargoes were not properly packaged, weighed or tied down. Plane instruments were being wrecked by fine coal dust.

The technical problems were highlighted by one particularly embarrassing incident. Tunner had been presented with a magnificent gold, jewel-studded hunting watch in a velvet case by an old man who said that he wanted to give it to the pilots who were saving his beloved Berlin. Tunner promised to present it to the man who had made the most airlift flights so far. The presentation was to be made in Berlin on, ominously enough, Friday 13th August. A spea-

Tunner instilled a spirit of competition. The 100,000th ton of supplies to break the blockade is received and triumpantly noted

ker's platform, a band and a guard of honour were organised. But then, as Tunner flew into Berlin for the ceremony, the weather closed in. Rain flooded down. The tower controllers couldn't see the runway through the torrential downpour and the planes, unable to land, were stacked up in a twenty mile circle above Tempelhof airfield. Along with them was Tunner's plane. Eventually, through the radio chatter of the air-controllers and the pilots, Tunner's voice cut in, 'Get those God-damned planes out of here!' Every plane returned to its base in West Germany. As Tunner himself wrote later: 'It was damned embarrassing: the Commander of the Berlin airlift couldn't even get *himself* to Berlin'.

There was little Tunner could do about the weather, of course, but he could improve the performance of each aeroplane. For three days, officers locked themselves away with note-pads, string, models of aircraft and coathangers. They looped the string round rooms, hung the hangers from the string and model planes from the hangers and worked out an acceptable flight schedule. Putting the plans into effect was something else again.

The major problem was maintenance. Every plane needed a check every day, a more thorough inspection every fifty hours of flying time and, beside incidental repairs during operation, every aircraft required a complete overhaul every 200 hours of flight and total rebuilding after every 1,000 hours. This last was a fortnight-long operation in a factory.

Tunner created special alert crews ready to rush out in jeeps when forwarned of some special trouble by the pilot. Thus whether the pilot reported trouble with a propeller or carburetor or breaks there was always an expert waiting on the tarmac when the plane landed.

To the overall problem of the shortage of mechanics, Tunner found an easy solution: the Germans them-

selves. Previously, the no-fraternisation order had forbidden such co-operation, but Tunner approached Clay direct and gained his permission to lift the ruling. American service manuals were rapidly translated into German, a language school was set up and soon the airlift had more German mechanics than American. Next, an old Luftwaffe repair base was re-opened. It was called Oberpfaffenhofen and the Americans called it familiarly. 'Oberhuffin-puffin,' or more usually 'Obie'.

For the fortnight's rebuilding the planes were flown back to the USA and serviced in commercial factories or at Navy and Air Force bases. In the States, the flow of tools, spare parts, and reconditioned engines could be organised on an efficient basis.

Training, too, was reorganised. New pilots were trained for the airlift operation at a special training school set up at Great Falls, Montana, where an exact duplicate of the approach to Tempelhof was established. When the new crews arrived in Germany they felt they had done it all before. In this way, with up to twenty-nine fresh crews a week being provided, it was eventually possible to rotate the men who had been too long on temporary duty.

As a result of the embarrassing incident over Tempelhof, Tunner ruled that if any pilot missed his landing on the first approach he was to turn into the centre corridor and return home. He also made a stern ruling about the weather: pilots *had* to land if the cloud ceiling was greater than 400 feet and they could see more than a mile, and they were *forbidden* to land if the ceiling and visibility were less.

Occasionally pilots found that their return flights, too, were dogged by bad weather and they had to fly on from Rhein-Main or Wiesbaden to one of the alternative bases, Vienna or Marseille. Once a crew mistook their bearings, flew on and on until they spotted an airfield, and landed only to find that they had come down in Prague, well behind the Iron Curtain. They were greeted with delight by the Czech airforce officers who threw a party for them and made them stay the night. They were hardly asleep when they were shaken awake by the American military attaché who told them that the Russians had found out that they were there and they had better get out quickly. The Czechs had meanwhile refuelled the aircraft and they took off safely.

Also as a result of Black Friday, as Tunner called the 13th August debacle, twenty civil air traffic controllers were brought over from the United States to do duty at Tempelhof and two radar systems were brought over which allowed the planes to be talked down. This technique, known as Ground Control Approach (GCA), was a system already in use in civil airlines but which normally involved stacking other planes while fifteen or twenty minutes were devoted to bringing a single plane down. In Berlin, GCA plane landings were made on the planes' regular three minute landing schedule.

Ground Controllers could thus guide the planes over the beacons, tell them when to turn and at what height they were flying. The final run-in would sound something like this: 'You are now six miles east of the runway, approaching the glide path; start rate of descent at 550 feet per minute, your azimuth [direction relative to the landing path] is good, your rate of descent is good; now correct left to 261 degrees; you are now coming back on azimuth, correct back right to 264 degrees; you are drifting above the glide path; you are 500 feet high, increase your rate of descent,' and so on until: 'You are on the glide path, you are one half mile from touchdown, you are on the glide path, your azimuth is good, you are now approaching the end of the runway, you are on the glide path, you are fifty feet over the runway, take over and land.' There were, of course, always those pilots quite happy to break the regulations. The legendary B T O'Reilly, who could reputably fly without the aid of instruments, was said to have taken his Lancaster to Berlin through fog when nothing else in the whole of Germany was flying. He simply collected his crew and arrived at the airfield at Wunstorf after a night out and took off without waiting for clearance and thus without his flight being recorded at all. The cloud was low but this did not worry him since he preferred flying at ground level anyway, presumably to find his way. Arriving at Gatow he ploughed through some thick fog until he found a gap, spotted the airfield and landed. As soon as the Lancaster's load had been dumped he took off, again without bothering about clearing control and found his way back to Wunstorf.

The next step was to co-ordinate the American and British airlifts. The British bases of Celle and Fassberg were half an hour's flying time closer to Berlin than the American base at Rhein-Main. Besides, the British were still flying many twin-engined Dakotas which could not carry nearly as much as the four-engined American C54s. A combined administration with centralised control would dramatically increase efficiency.

The British commander, Sir Arthur Sanders, was naturally a little reluctant. It would mean handing over the top command to the Americans, since they would be taking eighty per cent of the carrying capacity. However, he saw the necessity and agreed.

The operation went even more smoothly. It now had the services of 280 planes divided into four blocks. Time and motion men studied every aspect of the operation: loading and unloading, fuelling, briefing, dispatching. Soon ten tons of cargo could be stowed in a C54 in twenty minutes and removed in thirty minutes. Scores of charts in the control centre kept tabs on every

British Air Minister Arthur Henderson
on a tour of inspection

conceivable part of the operation:
turn around times, engine availa-
bility, use of aircraft, flying hours,
etc.

To supply the airlift was an
operation in itself, and one of incredible complexity. There was a
Land Rear Air ·Supply Organisation
which organised the arrival of the
the supplies by railway and truck
at the airfield, where they were
shifted on to lorries for loading – one
three-ton truck carried one Dakota
load, two three-tonners filled one
York – and there was a Sea Rear Air
Supply Organisation which loaded
flying boats on the river at
Finkenwerder, where supplies arrived
by barge. Germans did the loading
while the aircraft was serviced under
the supervision of Air Despatchers
(Army) or Air Maintenance Assistants
(RAF).

Efficiency was very much a question
of packaging, which at first was
hopelessly inadequate. Supplies
arrived in sacks, which kept on
splitting. Flour, for instance, used to
arrive in 220-pound sacks which
exhausted the German loaders. Dried
egg reached the bases in 250-pound
drums – impossible to handle. Small
tins would arrive packed in bulky
wooden boxes. Many supplies arrived
in 200-pound units which were too big
for one man to handle – but which two
men could not get through the
relatively narrow aircraft doors side
by side. Soon all this was changed.
An army Time and Motion Study
Group laid down that all units should
be between one and two cubic feet,
that there should be no cylinders and
no sacks.

All sorts of plans were suggested to
overcome the inefficiencies of loading
odd supplies into the aircraft,
including end loading with power

River police and British MPs waiting
for the arrival of flying boats

C-74 in the foreground, C-47 landing

equipment, gliders to be released over
Berlin, and air-dropping coal. (The
last of these was not a bad idea, but it
was abandoned because of the diffi-
culty of making accurate drops in bad
weather and because of the traffic
congestion that would ensue over
Berlin.)

By the end of August 5,000 tons a
month was being flown into the
beleagured city, 500 tons above the
minimum level estimated for survival,
and in October the minimum level
was raised to 5,620 tons a month.

What was the theoretical upper
limit? The large C74 gave the answer.

It had a carrying capacity of twenty-
five tons. Making six trips in
twenty-four hours, it could carry
150 tons into Berlin every day. More of
these aircraft were on the way but
they were not yet ready for delivery.
Tunner was fond of speculating what
a full fleet of 300 or so C74s could do.
He worked out that they would easily
ferry 24,000 tons of supplies a day into
Berlin, far more than the normal
requirements of the city. There were,
apparently, grounds for optimism.

The Russians did little to stop the
airlift. They would sometimes indulge
in a little anti-aircraft practice on
targets towed into the edges of the
flight corridors, and occasionally

Russian planes buzzed the transports. They once flashed search-lights into the eyes of the pilots as they took off from Berlin. They could have done much more: they could have jammed radio communications or put up barrage balloons, but they were obviously not going to risk escalating the crisis.

Tunner thought the Russian's failure to take more extreme measures was due to their conviction that the airlift would fail. After all, Hitler had tried to supply the German army at Stalingrad by air. The Germans had needed to supply 300 tons a day but had never succeeded in delivering more than ninety. It seemed reason-able to assess the Berlin airlift's chances of success in the light of this earlier attempt by the same terms. In addition, the Russians had not yet mastered instrument flying and were sure that the long German winter, with its almost continuous blanket of cloud would halt operations.

Peculiar problems arose which demanded their own peculiar solutions. One of these was icing, a problem overcome in flight by the operation of de-icers which worked off the engines and vibrated the ice apart as soon as it formed. On the ground, however, the engines were idle, and there was no efficient and ready-made way of dealing with the

An iron girder airlifted to Berlin. It was
necessary to 'slice up' heavy machinery
for air transport, the pieces being
welded together again on arrival

build-up of ice on planes standing on
the runway. A sergeant devised an
easy answer; he pointed out that there
were a couple of decommissioned jet
fighter planes available. Why not, he
thought, put the jets on small trucks
and use them as enormous hot air
blowers? It worked perfectly. On cold
days, the trucks carrying the howling
jets trundled slowly backwards and
forwards in front of the large transport
planes, which then took off with warm
wings.

A rather more massive and dramatic
problem was posed by the need to
shift large scale earth-moving
equipment into Berlin to help build
the runways. At Tempelhof they
needed graders, bulldozers, rollers,
scrapers, stone crushers. But all
such things had been removed by the
Russians and the machinery was too
vast to fit even into the giant C74.
Then someone remembered a civilian
called H P Lacomb. Lacomb was a
welder by profession, but during the
war he had been involved in building
up an airbase in Brazil. Earth-moving
equipment had been needed there as
well. Lacomb, a genius with an
oxy-acetyline torch, had the answer.

Tempelhof, where he put the whole machine back together again. Soon he had a whole school of welders working for him and there was now nothing too big to move into Berlin. His men carved up a mammoth generator and sent it in in pieces. It was the largest in Berlin and the current it provided at least partially overcame one of the worst hardships of the blockade.

Towards the end of the summer, with most of the initial problems solved, Berlin now faced another shortage: airports. Neither Tempelhof nor Gatow could be expanded, but there was an ideal location in the French Zone, a rolling field near Tegel, which had once been used as a training site for the German army. Normally it would not be a difficult engineering job but conditions were far from normal. Lacomb's team could carve up enough equipment and fly it in, but concrete would take up valuable food space in the aircraft.

There was however a substitute for concrete, a material of which there was a superabundance in bombed Berlin: broken brick. The next problem was to get the brick from the city to the field – and ten million bricks were needed. The call went out to the Berliners themselves and 17,000 – forty per cent of them women – responded. They were all sorts: labourers and ex-army officers, scientists and teachers, society women and peasants.

Work started on 5th September, and it was planned to take four months over the Tegel runway. It looked as if it would take at least that: to level Tegel's rolling grassland would take bricks enough to build ten city blocks. After seeing the Berliners at work, however, the estimate was lowered by a fortnight. In fact, the task was completed after only two months, and on 5th November the first plane landed at Tegel. It became the chief terminal for British tankers flying in fuel – Diesel, Kerosene and Gasoline – for which four large under-

He carved the monster machines apart into jigsaw pieces, each of which would fit into a plane. Then he flew in with the various pieces and welded them all back together again. With the help of the FBI, Lacomb was found working at a tiny airport in the Mid-West. He was at once whipped into Rhein-Main, complete with all his torches.

He soon displayed his skill: arriving at the base, he approached a bulldozer, walked round it thoughtfully, marked it into sections with chalk and then, over two days, carved it into bits. Each bit was light enough to fit into the C74, and after it was loaded, Lacomb boarded as well and flew to

Berliners at work on the Tegel runway

ground storage tanks had been built.

There was only one main obstruction to the Tegel airway: the transmission tower of the Berlin Radio Station. It was unquestionably a danger and ought to be removed, but the situation was a strange one: the radio station itself was in the British Sector, its tower was in the French Sector and the operation of the station was controlled by the Russians, who ignored requests for its removal.

Eventually the French Commandant in Berlin, General Ganeval, devised a radical but effective solution. He invited the twenty Americans stationed at Tegel to a mysterious meeting at his office. When they arrived, he locked the door and served them all champagne. Meanwhile, French engineers were placing demolition charges at the base of the tower. Suddenly a blast shook the building: the Americans rushed to the window in time to see the 200 foot tower slowly toppling to the ground.

The Russians, of course, protested vigorously but the Americans had a perfect alibi: they were under lock and key when it happened. The Russians could only blame the French, which was hardly as strong a political weapon as blaming the Americans and the British.

There were additional improvements at Tempelhof as well. Landing would be made much safer with good guide lights, but these could not be put out at ground level because of the buildings surrounding Tempelhof. They had to be placed on towers which were built out of the large perforated steel plates that had previously covered the Tempelhof airstrip.

The siting of these towers produced some paradoxical propaganda from the Russians. The only possible location for them was in a cemetery adjoining Tempelhof, and to build them graves had to be moved and the steeple of a small church removed.

Russian intransigence is dealt with effectively: the Berlin Radio Station transmission tower is dynamited by the French

The Russians had a field-day describing how the American warmongers were desecrating the graves of the sacred dead.

Loading the planes at the West German air bases also went from strength to strength. It took a miracle of organisation to arrange that all of the 500 trucks arriving every day with an assortment of one hundred different food stuffs and medicines, should have loads best suited to the shape of the aircraft, of the right tonnage and be at the right place at the right time.

All the work was proved worthwhile when the airlift organisers showed it was possible to beat even the German winter. On 1st November, the food ration was increased by twenty per cent to a level that was two hundred and twenty calories per day higher than the ration before the blockade started.

The first planes land at Tegel

The gamble pays off

The ration stayed high – despite the fact that November was one of the worst months, with the weather limiting flying to fifteen days out of thirty. Not that this factor deterred the pilferers. It was a full-time job checking up on this aspect of the airlift alone. At Gatow the man in charge was Captain W R Bateman, a plump, energetic officer. He and his men would make snap checks on the unloading teams as they walked back from the aircraft. Bateman would drive up in his jeep and his men would jump out, surround the workers and pat their pockets. On one occasion they found that a man had butter packed down the sides of his jack boots, and they discovered that a favourite trick among the German workers was to conceal flour and sugar in little bags suspended inside the trousers. In fact, precautions were not as stringent as they could have been in order not to alienate the German workers, but those that were caught were made examples of.

In September Bateman was involved in what could have been very serious trouble of a different kind. One of the foremen told him there was a riot brewing at a gate near the unloading strip. It appeared that one of the RAF Police Corporals on duty at the gate had asked to see the passes of the 300 workers who were coming to start their shift in the airfield. The workers laughed at his officious request and started pushing through the gate and climbing the fence on either side of it.

The Blockade is lifted

The corporal called up an armoured car and, as one of the crew was getting out of it, his sten-gun went off accidentally, shooting a young German worker through the foot. The workers were inscensed, quite naturally, and it took Bateman an hour to persuade them to go on with their shift.

This provided heady material for the Russian propagandists. On 19th September the Russian controlled *Neues Deutschland* headlined, 'slaves serving Anglo-Americans, dreadful treatment of German workers at Gatow'. 'One of the officers known as the Fat Captain [Bateman],' ran the report ominously, 'is well known for his unusual methods', and four days later another report suggested that the shooting had been a deliberate act of revenge for the pilfering that had been going on.

There were disasters, but very few. One of these occurred on 11th November 1948. It involved a Dakota and a pilot named Trezona, who came from the Cornish town of Eslick. Trezona was the only one of the pilots to take off that night who did not have instrument rating, but he was a very competent pilot and was placed as a precaution in the middle of a block of Dakotas with four rated pilots in front of him and four behind. The flight left Lübeck safely and landed in Gatow. There a soldier who had been . given compassionate leave hitched a lift with Trezona, and although the pilot was not cleared to carry passengers he agreed to do so and left at once. This now put him in

97

Lieutenant Gale Halverson, originator of operation 'Little Vittles'

the front of the return flight. On the way back the weather closed in. The approach was over the Russian Zone, which ended at the edge of the airfield. Five miles out the planes were at 15,000 feet losing 300 every mile. Trezona called in at six miles out: 'King Peter 223, turning finals, six miles'. That was the last anyone heard from King Peter 223. Several times the Lübeck controller called to him: 'Hello King Peter 223, King Peter 223, overshoot, overshoot'. When the second plane was about three-and-a-half miles from touchdown, flying control heard the pilot cry out, 'Jesus! the whole place is lit up, there's a ruddy great fire here'. King Peter 223 had crashed and was burning in the Russian Zone. No one discovered why, the Russians never said and the four people on board were killed.

The decision by the officer commanding at Gatow, Lieutenant Colonel Graham, to introduce generators to heat the British staff offices resulted in the perpetration of

a very odd error, which could have proved fatal. The generators were gathered from the British Zone at Wunstorf ready to be shipped into Berlin. On the sides of the crated generators were painted the figures '2,000', and it was assumed that this meant 2,000 lbs, which meant that two generators would fit comfortably into each York. But then it proved impossible to fit more than one into each York. After several had been flown safely into Gatow, loading staff decided that the crates were unnecessary. The sides and top were taken off each one, leaving the generators on their base plates. New instructions were drawn for the loading of the generators and a two-and-a-half ton crane was drawn up and began to haul on one of the machines to get it into position. The crane tipped gently forwards but the generator did not budge. Only then did the British find out that the generators, far from weighing 2,000 pounds each, weighed 8,000. If two of them could have been got into a York the plane would probably never have left the ground or would have crashed soon after take-off.

To the Berliners, perhaps the best known personality of the airlift was a prematurely bald, twenty-seven-year-old bachelor from Garland, Utah – Lieutenant Gale Halverson. His love for the Berlin children produced one of the best Berlin newspaper stories of the airlift. He noticed that wherever he had gone in Africa, Italy and South America, queues of children had formed behind him begging him for sweets and chewing gum. In Berlin this did not happen. He described his first meeting with the children: 'Their English is about as bad as my German but I saw there was something missing. Finally I realised what it was: those kids hadn't begged for a single thing. They just lacked the brass other kids have. So I told them to be down at the other end of the runway next day and I would drop them some gum and some candy.'

Which is exactly what he did, parachuting chocolate bars and chewing gum down on handkerchiefs.

When the press heard about this they rapidly dubbed his operation 'Little Vittles,' and the habit rapidly spread to other pilots, until many of them were spending much of their free time making little parachutes for the next day's drop.

The publicity given to Operation 'Little Vittles' in America brought in a flood of sweets, many of them already packaged and attached to parachutes. From then on, the crowd of children in the cemetery at the end of the runway became a permanent feature of the airlift.

The campaign to look after Berlin's children acquired another dimension with the arrival one afternoon, to the amazement of the watching crowds, of a camel loaded with sweets. The camel, named Clarence, had been brought together with a donkey from North Africa by an enterprising, publicity-conscious American Lieu-

Anticipating Halverson's arrival

tenant named Butterfield. Using Clarence as a symbol, the Air Force organized a project, naturally known as the 'Camel Caravan,' to collect food and other gifts from West Germany. The campaign was an enormous success, despite the fact that Clarence himself didn't last long: his friend the donkey lashed out at him one day, broke his leg, and he had to be shot. Nothing daunted, Lieutenant Butterfield acquired another camel, and the campaign continued.

The response from the whole West was fantastic, beginning with West Germany. There a special two-Pfennig stamp was required in addition to the regular postage, the proceeds of which were used to buy supplies for Berlin. Westphalia and Saxony went on a one day fast and contributed the day's food ration, plus 100,000 tons of coal, to Berlin. Bremen donated twenty million cigarettes, the Bavarian Red

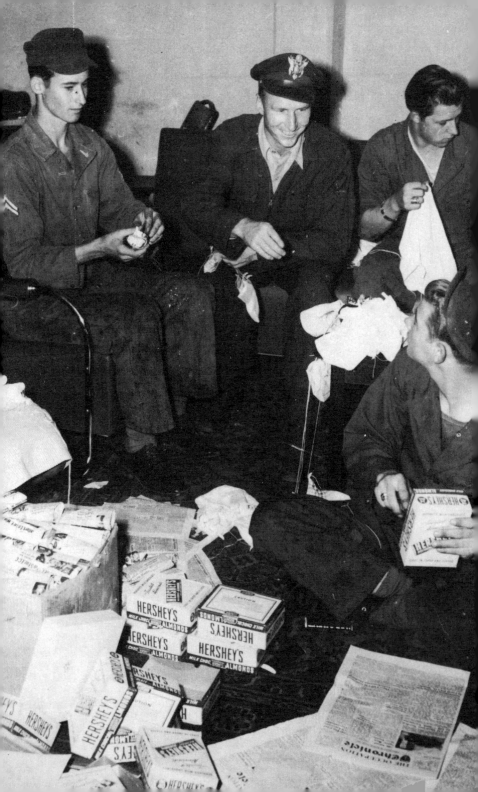

Cross sent in a ton of medicine, Schleswig Holstein sent two million pine tree seedlings to replace the trees bombed or cut down in Berlin. From America, trade unionists sent 20,000 food parcels and Stanford University sent fifteen tons of food to West Berlin universities. There was even an offer, not taken up, from the National Institute of Diaper Services of America to fly in 12,000 nappies a week and fly out dirty ones to be washed.

Perhaps the prize for originality goes to one enterprising airlift squadron. A squadron spokesman telephoned the cartoonist, Al Capp, creator of Li'l Abner, who had recently devised a character called the Schmoo. This pear-shaped roly-poly fellow was remarkable: he could turn himself into anything to help people out of a fix – a chicken dinner, bricks, dresses,

Little parachutes are prepared for the children; Lieutenant Halverson centre

The campaign to collect gifts from the Western world for Berlin's children is almost embarrassingly successful

shoes, gold. The point of the call was to get the cartoonist's permission to use his new creation in their plan. Having obtained Capp's agreement, the men of the squadron bought one hundred packages from CARE (Co-operative for American Remittances to Everywhere), distributed them to CARE offices in Berlin and then acquired an equal number of inflated balloon Schmoos, which were then being sold as toys in the United States. The Schmoos were then floated down near Tempelhof, each one bearing a card inscribed: 'Hello, I'm a Schmoo, take me to a CARE office and you will see how fast I can change into a CARE package'. In return presents flowed from the Berliners. There was a stream of women, children and old people crowding to the airports to press a

range of presents on the pilots. These included puppies, mufflers, paintings, china, heirlooms, pastry, books.

The incoming cargo also included a constant stream of VIPs. Of the 5,260-ton daily quota thirty tons was reserved for 'people'. This meant there were on an average about 350 people a day flying into Berlin. These included, from England, Prime Minister Clement Attlee, the Foreign Minister Ernest Bevin, Anthony Eden, and the RAF Chief Air Marshal Tedder. Attlee arrived in a gale force wind with a

The American sector contributes boots for the needy. General Clay's wife (in furs) lends her support.

A Schmoo brings presents

load of coal, and descended in a cloud of black dust on to the tarmac. Bevin, while on a tour of inspection, spotted a chart labelled, 'Organisational Chart'. 'What kind of a word is that?' he growled, 'there's no such word in the English language as "organisational!" You Americans made it up!'

From America came the Secretary of the Air Force, Stewart Symington, whose visit proved particularly welcome. Chatting to a grimy mechanic at Rhein-Main he learned that the staff at the base were extremely disgruntled. 'See these,' the mechanic said, holding up a pair

Above: Clement Attlee and General Clay at Tempelhof. *Below:* Ernest Bevin arrives at Tempelhof

Above: Sir Anthony Eden in Berlin. *Below:* Air MarshalTedder inspecting Tegel airport

Stewart Symington and, right, General Vandenberg

of pliers, a wrench and a screwdriver, 'I bought them myself in Germany'. Symington at once commissioned Tunner to provide a report on what was needed and when he got home he requisitioned better housing and large quantities of much needed supplies.

Another arrival was Bob Hope, whose visit caused a flurry of controversy. He came to put on a Christmas show which was billed weeks in advance as a show for the airlift personnel. In fact, the organisation was undertaken by the American Air Force – not by the airlift command. As a result, the two shows were scheduled for Wiesbaden, far from the Rhein-Main air base, and for a spot in Berlin almost inaccessible to the airlift personnel at Tempelhof. Tunner immediately demanded that all mention of the airlift be dropped from the advance publicity. Such a step would, of course, negate the

purpose of Bob Hope's visit, and three more shows were quickly scheduled at airlift bases.

Thanks to the airlift it was possible to survive the winter in Berlin, but there was nothing pleasant about it. The city had two Governments, two kinds of money, two sorts of newspaper, two totally contrary radio stations and one third of the city was on relief. People waited endlessly, for the electricity to come on, for the distribution of tobacco, for fuel, for food.

As winter set in the cold became a personal enemy for every Berliner. The ration of coal for most families was no more than twenty-five pounds for the whole winter and few people yet had warm clothes.

Still, people put up with it. The City Government even rejected an Allied suggestion that an extensive wood on the West side of the city, the Grünewald, be cut down, for it was a wood of which Berliners were particularly fond.

Above: Bob Hope arrives to perform at a Christmas show. *Below:* Berliners queue for their free ration of coal

Exchanging money on the black market

Secreting Western currency (illegal in
East Berlin) before entering the
Russian sector

A particular annoyance for Berlin through the winter was the two-currency system of East and West Marks. Both were legal tender but the West Marks were by far the stronger. Everybody wanted to be paid in West Marks, and though technically on a par, this was soon abandoned and the rate of exchange set at four East Marks to one West Mark. The currency split produced a strange crop of problems for anyone who worked on one side of the border and lived on the other. East Berliners who worked in the West being partly paid in West German Marks would take their wage packets to the Black Market, buy a larger number of East German Marks and return home with inflated pay packets having allowed their wages to inflate the Black Market. West Berliners who worked in the East simply did not have enough buying power to live, so an exchange office was set up on the Border at which West Berliners could exchange their East Berlin Marks for West Marks at an artificially balanced rate. Both situations were bad for the economy.

At one point this led to a comic piece of irony: speakers on the communist-controlled Radio Berlin demanded to be paid in West Marks – and these were the same people who were broadcasting the communist propaganda line that East Marks were, in fact, as valuable as West Marks! The situation was only sorted out in the spring of 1949 when the Western powers at last gave up the hope of a single currency in Berlin and declared the West Mark to be the only legal tender in the Western sectors.

The split between the two sides hardened constantly. When the Soviets evicted forty known democrats from their houses in the Eastern Sector, the West Berlin press insisted that forty communists be ejected from the Western sectors. East Berlin policemen who tried to search West Berliners in the Russian Sector were several times driven off by an irate crowd of West Berliners. Soviet propaganda continued in full swing directed mainly against the Americans. 'What has American imperialism to offer us in the way of culture?' the radio would ask; 'Is it the boogey-woogey culture of sensational and immoral films which appeal to the lowest instincts?'

The Russians clamped down in their own sector. They reintroduced the Nazi system of house wardens, minor officials who were supposed to report on the feelings of the occupiers in a single apartment house or group of private houses. In connection with Russian Army manoeuvres in East Germany, a ring of tanks was

Volkspolizei parading

assembled facing Berlin, and the *Volkspolizei* – the people's police force – was increased to 400,000. As a result rumours – no-one knew if they were true or not – spread that the Russians were planning a takeover of West Berlin. Controls were introduced on the underground line running between the Eastern and Western sectors. Check points were set up on the East-West boundaries. In an attempt to clamp down on the food and coal that was smuggled back and forth ditches and barricades were established to funnel the flow of traffic through the check points. They were almost useless. There were too many points, like the vast apart-ment buildings which straddled the border, which could not be adequately patrolled.

The Black Market became so extensive that the Russians them-selves made use of it, sanctioning shops in the Eastern Sector that specialised in luxury goods – food, textiles, cigarettes – at ridiculously high prices.

There were some positive gains to the blockade. Robbery and house-breaking had become less frequent, the incidence of serious diseases such as tuberculosis, typhoid and diph-theria had declined. In short, life was

hard but bearable. It was drab, trying, exhausting and grim, but the Berliners retained a dogged humour, a sense of detachment and of scepticism, a curious sardonic confidence, and those in the Western sector were borne up by the knowledge that they would be far worse off in Russian hands: 'If there's got to be a blockade,' ran a current quip, 'it's better to be blockaded by the Soviets and fed by the Americans; just imagine if it was the other way round'.

There was also a much needed feeling of solidarity; family and neighbourhood groups were bound together by stronger ties than ever before. An old man, recalling the atmosphere of the airlift later, told how people would gather in groups in the evening in thick clouds of cigarette smoke: 'Jokes and songs always came into their own and the airlift planes roaring through the night sang the base in perfect time'. There was the feeling of comradeship they had once found in an air-raid shelter but without the same worry and fear, and increasingly there was pride. Pride in their own fortitude, in being accepted as full partners by the Western Allies, in being praised by the outside world. Largely as a result of the airlift the Berliners could forget the feeling of rejection they had felt after defeat, and the humiliation of occupation. Almost overnight they had ceased to be treated as conquered people – their former enemies helped them and even praised them. Many people thought that a little physical suffering was not too great a price to pay for restoration of self respect and human dignity.

In an essay competition held later by a newspaper, *Der Abend*, many Berliners expressed the surprise, delight and even embarrassment they felt at being regarded with affection by the Allies and at being thought of as heroes. As one Berlin housewife wrote, 'Praise helped to give a stiff backbone and I walked proudly

Temporary home for the homeless

through the streets. I was helping to write a proud page in the history of Berlin housewives.' A report on the city's morale summarised this odd mixture of emotions. 'Berliners smiled when some leading personality of the West spoke over the radio and praised the courage and steadfastness of the Berliners. But in this smile there was something akin to embarrassment and pride. We didn't know whether we were really heroes or not, and if we are heroes it isn't because we have done so much. In the last analysis we are heroes because we are afraid of the Soviets and because we happen to live in Berlin.'

With the next elections due to take place, two years after the 1946 ones, the split between the two halves of the city became even more pronounced. The Socialist Unity party declared that it would boycott the election and Kotikov made it clear that the only conditions under which the Russians would permit a city-wide election amounted to Soviet control of the entire city. The election would therefore be held in the Western sectors only. This time communist disruption tactics were not very successful. Though party workers were kidnapped by Eastern Sector police and Socialist Unity squads hurled stink bombs at democratic party meetings, the communists now found themselves facing squads of young men as eager for a fight as they were. Communist hecklers on the whole got very short shrift.

Once again the communists drummed out their propaganda slogans, trying to convince the West Berliners that to vote at all would irrevocably split the city and be a vote of confidence in the condition that existed in Berlin. Communist newspapers carried notices such as the following: 'Housewives in the West – do you want people to think you are satisfied with electricity rationing, with the tiny gas ration, with dark and cold homes? On 5th December, get even with those who want to split Berlin.

Don't vote!' There was an appalling radio jingle which went roughly as follows:
'Don't be lured by promises sweet,
Think of the dried potatoes you have to eat.
Think of all the cut down trees
And the dark, cold rooms in which you freeze.
Don't vote for the candidates like a dunce,
Whose parties have already betrayed you once.'

Despite all this frantic propaganda the West Berliners flocked to the polls on 5th December. Eighty-five per cent of the 1,500,000 eligible voters cast ballots, and the Social Democrats won an absolute majority of 64·5 per cent.

After this result became public the initiative in West Berlin was more clearly with the West, a fact that was highlighted by a counter blockade instituted by the Western Allies. As of January 1949, the American and British zones were closed to vehicles travelling to and from East Germany. The communists were made to pay in West Marks for anything that they bought in West Berlin. They even had to scrape up 185,000 West Marks for twenty-five tons of bronze that was to decorate a memorial for the Russians who had died in the battle for Berlin.

By January too it was clear that the airlift had beaten the blockade. 225 American planes and about one hundred British ones were landing anything up to 5,500 tons a day from eight bases: Wunstorf, Fassberg, Celle, Schleswigland, Fuhlsbüttel, Lübeck, Wiesbaden and Rhein-Main.

In that month bad weather so reduced flying time that an acute shortage of coal developed while stockpiled food was only sufficient for a month. Scarcely one week's coal supply remained. At this point

Results of the December 1948 elections are displayed as they come in

the Russians were still gambling that the West would fail and the Americans took a calculated risk. Food was cut back in favour of coal. Within a few days the supply of coal had been raised to the three week level and food stocks were reduced to about the same. The gamble paid off: the weather broke and the winter was as good as beaten. On 18th February, there arrived in Berlin the one millionth ton of airlifted supplies, and the Secretary of State, Dean Acheson, marked the occasion with a telegram of congratulations to General Clay.

President Truman recorded with satisfaction, 'Germany, which had been waiting passively to see where it should cast its lot for the future, was veering towards the cause of the Western nations'.

Relative luxuries began to arrive in Berlin; jam, varieties of cheese, enough paper to print books, glass, cement, new tools. As a result it became possible for planes to leave Berlin carrying goods manufactured in the city. In January one and a half million electric light bulbs were exported in crates marked 'Made in Blockaded Berlin'. A few small electric trains were exported to the Ruhr coal mines and became the basis of an exaggerated news story that Berlin was making trains to mine the coal which was then flown back into the city.

The airlift had now become almost part of the emotional make-up of the Berliners. It was the first subject of discussion and the most important news item in the papers. Records broken made people happy; when the tonnage figures sank, they were depressed. As a Berliner later said, the continual sound of engines was 'the most beautiful music to our ears'.

Things were going so well, indeed, that General Tunner even felt that the personnel were becoming too complacent and needed shaking up. For Easter 1949 he ordered an all out bid to establish a new airlift record. 10,000 tons of coal was his target, and when it was proclaimed on the Saturday before Easter, the announcement on the notice-boards drew sceptical whistles from the men. Easter was fine that year and everybody felt the pressure of competition. The English bases at Celle and Fassberg, always great competitors with each other, both ran ten per cent or more over quota and as the last plane came in at noon on Easter day after twenty-four hours of all-out effort, it bore the jubilant note painted in red on its side, 'Tons – 12,941, Flights – 1,398'. That day the airlift had averaged almost a trip a minute and transported the equivalent of 1,250 freight trains, all without a single accident or injury.

This was more than just a dramatic Easter gift. It showed the Russians that the city could, if necessary, be

Above: Proud RAF at Gatow. Below: Luxuries begin to arrive at last
Right: Another milestone: blockaded Berlin exports her own manufactures

A libation of Coke to celebrate the airlift's birthday

maintained on a normal basis without ground transport at all. It also showed that having come successfully through the winter, the city could survive under any conditions. The summer months ahead offered no particular problems. These facts, on top of the December election, effectively punctured communist policy and spelt an end to the blockade.

A hint that the Russians would be amenable to discussions about the blockade came from Stalin himself in an interview with the European Manager of the International News Service, Kingsbury Smith. The counter blockade set up by the Americans and the British in Berlin provided him with the *quid pro quo* he needed. 'The Soviet Union,' he said, 'sees no obstacles to lifting transport restrictions on the understanding, however, that transport and trade restrictions introduced by the three powers should be lifted simultaneously.'

Truman and Dean Acheson noticed when they studied the report that for the first time the Berlin blockade was not tied to the question of currency. Was this, they asked tentatively, an accidental omission? No said the Russian Ambassador, Jacob Malik, the omission was 'not accidental'. Therefore negotiations went forward rapidly, if secretly, not even General Clay being told that they were in progress.

There was little argument. Russia wanted a meeting of the Council of Foreign Ministers to discuss the whole German question, America said that that was not possible while the blockade was in progress. Russia replied that if a date for the meeting of the Council of Foreign Ministers was set the blockade would be lifted in advance of that meeting. It was agreed.

On 5th May an official statement was issued in Washington, Moscow, London and Paris announcing the lifting of all communication, transport and trade restrictions as of 12th May 1949.

At midnight on 11th May the checkpoint on the Autobahn leading out of West Berlin looked like London's Trafalgar Square on New Year's Eve. Hundreds of people, many of them in evening dress, danced in the road, lighted by car headlights. They were waiting for the first cars and lorries to reach Berlin from East Germany. As it happened the first vehicle proved to be a carload of American newsmen, but they were soon followed by the first of a line of flower-covered trucks.

The next day a new era dawned. Schools were closed and everybody went on a buying spree that was to last for days. Electricity flowed into the city again and people delighted in flicking on and off their light switches. Prices tumbled. Wholesalers in West Germany shipped anything they could into the capital. Black marketeers were promptly put out of business.

At a special meeting of the city assembly, Ernst Reuter, speaking to the assembly, mentioned the forty-eight American and British pilots who had lost their lives in air crashes during the blockade. Everyone present rose to their feet in tribute. A resolution was passed that the plaza in front of the Tempelhof airfield be renamed 'Airlift Place' (*Platz der Lüftbrucke*). Reuter concluded the meeting with a ringing tribute to Clay himself: 'In

Negotiating for the lifting of the blockade; left to right, Alexander Cadogan, Jacob Malik, Philip Jessup and Jean Chauvel

Festivities at the reopening of the Autobahn

our great demonstrations in the summer of the past year we called on the world for help, the world heard our cry . . . the memory of General Clay will never fade in Berlin. We know for what we have to thank this man (prolonged stormy applause) . . . we will never forget what he has done for us.' Three days later Clay returned to America. In his four years in Berlin he had seen Germany rise from the depths of defeat to find its place as a living symbol of Western democracy, a bastion standing against the advancing waves of communist expansion. In recognition of his achievement, 250,000 Berliners crowded to the airport to see him off. With his departure, the Allied military administration of Germany ended. Throughout West Germany and Berlin military government and officials were replaced by civilian administrators.

Meanwhile in West Germany the Berlin blockade had had another effect unplanned by its instigators: it had hastened the unification of the three Western occupation zones into present day West Germany. The Western Allies had been understandably hesitant about this idea, but the coming of the blockade dramatically indicated the price which might have to be paid if Western Germany was not unified.

Despite the settlement, however, the planes came flying in just the same. End-of-the-war trust of Russia had given way to such extreme distrust that the airlift was kept going just in case, building up a reserve of 300,000 tons of food. The month after the blockade was officially over was, in fact, the airlift's busiest month, and it didn't completely phase out until September.

The whole operation had cost the British seven and the Americans seventeen planes. Forty-eight men had died in crashes and another

Berliners rush to celebrate the lifting of the blockade

Airlift officers and crew march through London

thirty in accidents on the ground. This, though tragic, was an incredible safety record considering the number of flights – 276,926. And altogether 2,323,067 tons of supplies had been flown in.

There was some dispute as to the cost of the airlift. The American business magazine *Fortune* described the operation as 'A Rolls Royce delivery service to the worlds biggest poor house'. Figures of 230 million dollars were mentioned as estimates of the cost – about one hundred dollars per ton of food. In modern terms, it was not even particularly expensive, but anyway the cost was irrelevant. Berlin had become a symbol for all of Europe and the Western Allies commitment to its defence was a symbol of its will to defend Western Europe from further extensions of the communist empire. As *Life* magazine wrote in an editorial: 'Surrender would be a confession that we really did not have the dignity and moral purpose we boasted'. The 'bridge in the sky' proved that the West was prepared to stand by its commitments.

When he visited Berlin in 1961, President Kennedy assessed Berlin's new situation: 'It is more than a showcase of liberty, a symbol, an island of freedom in a communist sea. It is even more than a link with the free world, a beacon of hope behind the Iron Curtain, an escape hatch for refugees.

'West Berlin is all of that but above all it has now become, as never before, a great testing place of Western courage and will, a focal point where our solemn commitments . . . and Soviet ambitions now meet in basic confrontation.'

Compared with later, more confused, struggles between the Western and Communist Worlds this confrontation was simple, straightforward, dramatic. The first round had been won. For another decade, Berlin was to remain a symbol of freedom, a bone stuck in the communist throat, until it was time to fight the next round.

125

Action and reaction

Rusian tanks in the Potzdamer Platz,
June 1953

For the next twelve years, Berlin remained the focal point of the cold war. For the West it was a bastion of democracy surrounded by a sea of communism. For the East bloc countries, especially Russia, it was a last remnant of capitalism and imperialism, a plague spot to be eradicated as soon as possible.

For all that time it was an open window from East to West and East Germans poured through it at a staggering rate, thus both weakening the economy of East Germany, now attempting to gain recognition for itself as an independent nation, and threatening Russia's newly established empire in Eastern Europe. Attracted by the consumer goods in West Berlin's shop windows, by the uncensored publications, the theatres, the cabarets and the libraries, tens of thousands of East Berliners came over each evening. They need only walk a few streets or take the underground to be in a position to leave communism behind them for good. Many did just that – something over 150,000 people a year – an intolerable drain on East Germany and a permanent invitation – in conjunction with a still-enduring hope of reunification, carefully fostered by the West – to unrest in Eastern Europe.

These forces came to a first, tragic climax in 1953 when East Berlin workers revolted. On 16th June newspapers called upon East Germans to raise their work norms voluntarily by ten per cent – and this at a time

Walter Ulbricht inspects his factory militia on Stalin Allee

when even a reasonably well paid construction worker had to put in an eight hour day to buy a pound of butter.

The uprising began quite spontaneously on Block 40 of Stalinallee when construction workers sat down on their site and refused to get on with the job. They grabbed an official banner, prepared in advance, and, angered at its slogan 'Block 40 raises its norms ten per cent', they crossed it out and scrawled their own: 'We demand a lowering of work norms'.

Holding it aloft workers, about eighty of them, marched down the street, intending to protest to government leaders. As they marched others dropped their tools and joined in the protest. The crowd, growing all the time, paraded down Unter den Linden, past the Soviet Embassy, towards the seat of government in the Wilhelmstrasse, chanting 'Berliners, join our ranks. We don't want to be slaves.'

When they reached the House of the Ministries, formerly Göring's Luftwaffe HQ and now the principal East German government building, the original eighty marchers had become 8,000. As they approached, every window of the building closed, and in front of each a metal gate clicked into place. The workers chanted their demands at the blank facade, demanding to see the Party chief, Walter Ulbricht, or the Prime Minister, Otto Grotewohl. Three minor officials eventually appeared, but they were shoved aside with shouts of 'This is a popular uprising; we want to be Free!' Then, demanding a general strike for the following day the demonstrators marched back the way they had come and dispersed.

When the American Sector radio broadcast the news of the protest and the proposed general strike, the effect was electric. The following day, all over East Germany, some 350,000 workers took to the streets, many of them passing round hastily-written handbills demanding freedom for the press, better living and working conditions and free elections.

Towards late morning Russian troops appeared in East Berlin and other cities. In East Berlin, crowds shouting 'Shame, shame' at soldiers and police were so dense that the tanks were forced to a halt. They set off again only when the newly arrived Soviet commandant, Major General Pavel Diprova, signalled them on and then slowly drew his index finger across his throat to show what would happen if they failed to move.

Suddenly shots were fired, whether by Russian troops or East German People's Policemen is unclear, and the shooting continued. The crowds scattered, but hundreds of young East Berliners continued to bombard armoured vehicles with stones. Much of this had happened within full sight of West Berliners, who stood horrified on the zonal boundary.

By evening the Soviets were in complete control. The death role for that one day was appallingly enough: 18 Soviet soldiers, 116 East German policemen and 267 demonstrators. But afterwards over 100 were executed for their parts in the revolt. Another 1,200 were imprisoned.

The uprising made several things brutally plain about the status of Berlin. The first was that Berlin was already a city divided by much more than the possession of rival administrations. This, of course, was implicit in the blockade, for although the Allies claimed to have saved Berlin, in fact they were saving *West* Berlin. They never had or claimed of have any authority over the territory of the Eastern Zone after the break-up of the four-power control system in

General Diprova on top of a T-34 tank rides through crowds of demonstrators

Scene of the uprising

March 1948.

Now the reality of the division became clear to all. For all the Western Allies' protestations that Berlin was still technically a four-power city, they would not and could not intervene in the Eastern Sector, even to aid revolt. It would have meant war, just as surely as an invasion of the Western sectors by Russian troops. There could be no doubting now that Berlin was a divided city and that there was nothing to stop Russia incorporating East Berlin into East Germany if and when they wished.

Neither the Soviet way of dealing with the revolt, nor the revolt itself, solved anything. West Berlin remained a bolt hole into West Germany from the East. In the twelve years between the end of the blockade in 1949 and the coming of the Wall in 1961, 2,800,000 East Germans fled, and perhaps another half million escaped into the West without registering with West German authorities. Thousands of her scientists, many of them of the highest calibre, left – 1,600 in 1958–61 alone. Three quarters of those who left were under forty-five, a quarter under twenty-five. The number of industrial apprentices in East Berlin dropped by half. 30,000 newly qualified students, 800 engineers and technicians, 800 judges and lawyers – all joined in the condemnation of their new regime by voting against it with their feet. In one *Pravda* interview, Ulbricht estimated that it cost East Germany 30,000 million marks in lost investment.

The strain on East Germany's economy was intolerable, even on quite non-doctrinaire grounds. A low-level economy meant poverty and political repression, and thus eventually even greater unpopularity for the regime. It was a vicious circle

Reception centre for refugees from the East

that Ulbricht was desperate to break.

But East Germany was still an occupation zone and it was Russia who held the reigns of power. From Moscow, Khrushchev, newly in power after Stalin's death in 1953, could see the Berlin problem in a wider context: for him it was one of many pieces with which he played on the chequerboard of international diplomacy, and for almost a decade after the East Berlin uprising he used it as such, controlling the heat of international diplomacy with a shrewdness that often verged on brilliance.

For five years he made no move, while politically and militarily Russia consolidated her strength. In 1956, with the crushing of two more uprisings – in Poland and Hungary – the communist hold tightened. Then, in 1957, Russia shattered the growing Western complacency by launching the first earth satellite, thus – in the eyes of the world – proving herself technologically in advance of

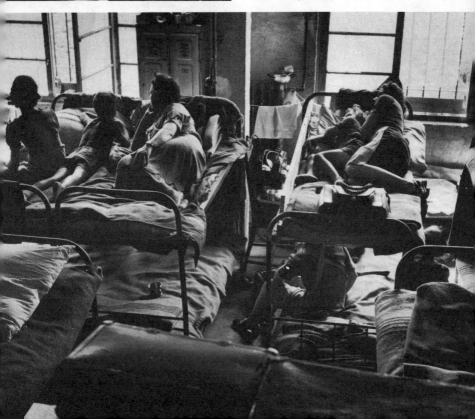

Left: Nikita Krushchev with Russian and German officials at the Soviet War Memorial in East Berlin. *Above:* Street scene during the uprising in Poland *Below:* Burning Soviet flags during the Hungarian revolt

General Henry Hodes

America. The shock to Western self-assurance gave Khrushchev the confidence he needed to reopen the Berlin question.

On 27th November 1958, he delivered an ultimatum to the United States, Britain and France demanding that the occupation of Berlin be terminated and that West Berlin be converted into a demilitarised 'free city' within six months. If, said Khrushchev, the West had not accepted his proposals within that time, then the Kremlin would conclude its own agreement with East Germany and end the occupation regardless. Berlin's role in the relation between the powers, he warned, with some degree of justification, 'compared to a smouldering fuse that had been connected to a powder keg. Only madmen can go to the length of unleashing another world war over the privileges of occupiers in West Berlin. If such madmen appear there is no doubt that straitjackets can be

found for them.'

It was a clever and confident move. It looked generous – could anyone really be against the idea of a 'free city'? It probed Western weakness in that it gave those prepared, after the launch of the Sputnik, to seek accommodation with Russia, an opportunity to make their feelings heard; it presupposed that the Western powers were in West Berlin still as occupiers, rather than as the defenders of the freedom of its $2\frac{1}{2}$ million inhabitants; and it also assumed that East Germany could be regarded as a sovereign state rather than as an occupied zone.

Khrushchev almost succeeded, but after a shaky start during which Western policy-makers found their feet, the West held firm. General Henry Hodes, Chief of the US Army in Europe, arrived in Berlin on a special inspection – three days after the note was received – a reminder to Berliners and Russia alike that there were 11,000 American troops on the ready in West Berlin. In London, Iain Macleod, Minister of Labour, stated decisively: 'Just because someone twitches the strings, doesn't mean that we should dance . . . We intend to stay there.'

But December brought the most decisive rebuff for Khrushchev when West Berlin itself went to the polls. An increased vote for the communists – the Socialist Unity Party were still recognised in West Berlin – would be interpreted universally as an endorsement of Khrushchev's proposals. A massive ninety-three per cent of the registered electors turned out to vote, and the result was a catastrophe for the communists. Willy Brandt's Socialists received fifty-two per cent and Adenauer's Christian Democrats thirty-seven per cent. These were followed by several other parties, and finally trailed the

communists, with two per cent, half the total they had received in 1954.

Now in a position of some strength, the West could insist on the legalities of the situation. They stated, in a reply to Khrushchev's note, on 31st December, that the three Western powers were in Berlin by right of conquest, not by kind permission of the Russians. Russia therefore had no authority to demand unilaterally changes to the status of West Berlin. No more than the West had any right to demand such changes in territory occupied by Soviet forces.

Faced with this resilience, the Russians backpedalled. They were not, they said, making an ultimatum for action in Berlin, but merely a deadline within which summit talks should begin. The West at first refused such high level talks, but took up the offer of negotiations at lower level, which which were held in Geneva the following year. Nothing was achieved.

By that time Khrushchev had won a rather more important diplomatic victory. He had been invited by Eisenhower to the States and had accepted. During his visit, he so often referred to the Berlin situation as 'abnormal' that the word had become accepted by the President himself. Abnormality implied the need for change and Moscow deduced from the acceptance of the word that there was reason to doubt Western firmness.

Khrushchev played for time, most spectacularly over the Paris Summit meeting. Using the U-2 incident, in which a high-flying spy-plane was shot down over Soviet territory, as an excuse, he banged on the table, denounced Eisenhower's perfidy and cancelled the meeting, but at the same time made no move to negotiate a peace treaty with East Germany. The situation was to be put on ice until after the coming Presidential election when he might pressure the new Administration to better advantage.

Meanwhile, Ulbricht, always

Gary Powers (left) whose plane was shot down over Russia, with a model of a U-2

US Ambassador, Walter Dowling

looking for the quick solution, kept up his pressure. He successfully demanded that a proposed meeting of the West German parliament in West Berlin, which the communists did not recognise as part of West Germany, be cancelled. He barred entry to the delegates to a convention of refugee organisations. He proclaimed that new passes would henceforth be needed by West Berliners travelling into the East Zone.

The clamp-down applied to some Allied personnel as well, after an apparently insignificant incident. One day, the American ambassador to West Germany, Walter Dowling, was driving through the Brandenburg Gate when his car was stopped by an East Berlin guard, who demanded to see his papers. Unthinkingly Dowling displayed them; he thus by implication recognised the right of the East Zone authorities to control the movement of Allied personnel into East Berlin. The following day, it was announced that all Allied diplomatic representatives would have to show their papers.

Thus, by the end of 1960, the East Germans had several gains: they had successfully challenged the Western right of unimpeded access to all parts of Berlin; they had curtailed the right of free movement for Berliners themselves; they had differentiated between West Berliners and West Germans – all important steps in the campaign to have both their own sovereign authority and the 'abnormality' of the Berlin situation recognised.

After Kennedy's accession to the Presidency in 1961, Khrushchev was offered an unexpected opportunity to renew pressure. In April, Kennedy received a humiliating blow when a group of rebel Cubans, backed by the United States, was crushed after a landing at the Bay of Pigs.

With US Administration in disarray Khrushchev offered to meet Kennedy, who accepted. A conference was fixed for June in Vienna. Khrushchev, fully aware that Kennedy was now negotiating within a framework of political failure, seized the opportunity to repeat and update his demands of November 1958: the Berlin situation must be 'normalised' by its conversion into a demilitarised free city. He added that both German states should meet and explore the possibilities of agreement within six months – a clear attempt to assert the existence of two sovereign and independent German states and thus end the agreed policy of German reunification based on free elections.

He lost no time in widening the chink he had found in Western armour. Six times in the month after the Vienna meeting he raised the question of Berlin in major speeches. He announced a massive twenty-five per cent increase in Russian military spending. Couching his demands in the language of peace, he convinced

Khrushchev and President Kennedy during their meeting in Vienna

many non-European nations that the city's status was anomolous, that it should be changed, that the West, by refusing to sign a treaty changing Berlin's situation, was standing in the way of lasting peace in Europe and thus threatening world war.

The Administration was divided and confused. There was no outright rejection of Khrushchev's demands. Senator Mike Mansfield pointed out to the Senate that the present US policy carried with it the American commitment to wage nuclear war over Berlin and doubted whether the country would be ready to accept this. Kennedy himself had been shattered by Khrushchev's intransigence. According to *Time* magazine, after the Vienna meeting, the President became 'moody, withdrawn, often fell into deep thought in the midst of festive occasions'. When, in a nationwide television broadcast, seven weeks after Vienna, Kennedy made a public reply, it seemed on the surface firm. It was certainly eloquent. He called West Berlin 'the great testing place of Western courage'. 'I hear it said', he went on, 'that West Berlin is military untenable. So was Bastogne. So, in fact, was Stalingrad. Any dangerous spot is tenable if men – brave men – make it so.' But throughout he mentioned only *West* Berlin, thus implying that a change in *East* Berlin's status would be acceptable.

Early in the following month Khrushchev decided the time was ripe to bring the crisis to a head. At a meeting of the Warsaw Pact heads of government, he yielded to Ulbricht's entreaties to close the border in East Berlin. The move was to take place a fortnight later. At once, to prepare the ground, Khrushchev stepped up his campaign. With another propaganda victory – German Titov's space-flight – to give him increased assurance, he unabashedly thrust the possibility of war at the West. A

The East Berlin watch on the border is intensified

clash over Berlin, he said, 'would mean a war between the two giants that would quickly develop into a thermo-nuclear conflict'. It was a clear warning against Western intervention over Berlin.

There could be no further delay in making changes in Berlin's status, he said. Not to go ahead with the signing of a peace treaty with East Germany would only encourage the West. They would inevitably demand the end of Socialism in East Germany, the annexation of lands given to Poland and Czechoslovakia in 1945, and then move on to demand the end of socialism in all Eastern Europe.

This was mere fantasy of course, but the situation in East Germany brooked no delay. The economy was already in a state of collapse. Despite the collectivisation of agriculture the previous year, supplies of basic commodities were still hopelessly inadequate. Production in industry was far below estimated requirements.

The situation was self-perpetuating. The existence of West Berlin as an escape hatch, the flow of refugees, the declining East German economy, the growing need for East Germany to clamp down, the campaign to prepare for this, the fear this caused among the East German Population – all this lead to a giddy spiral in the number of refugees – 30,000 fled in July alone, the imminent collapse of the East German economy and the possibility of a new and larger uprising.

Everyone knew a crisis was imminent. The 60,000 Eastern Zone residents who worked in the West were advised to find other jobs. Ulbricht clamped down on the movement of consumer goods between the zones. Refugees crowding in to the West Berlin reception centres brought details of border closure plans gleaned from local communist officials. Passenger rail links with the surrounding countryside were cut back. 'Flight from the Republic' became categorised as a crime punishable by two years imprisonment. East Berlin border

A crowd of West Berliners assembles at the Brandenburg Gate after the communist authorities announce new measures to stop escapes from the East

guards were increased six-fold.

At this point, many in the West saw that the situation demanded some dramatic solution. Senator Fulbright even stated categorically: 'I don't understand why the East Germans don't close their border. They have the right to close it.' When asked about the refugee problem Kennedy carefully avoided contradicting Fulbright's remarks. Khrushchev had succeeded: the crisis was now so clear cut, the threat of violence in East Germany now so obvious – with the real possibility thereafter of wider conflict – that the West would almost certainly acquiesce in the closure of the border.

On 13th August the communists moved into action. At a few minutes past midnight, teleprinters in Berlin began to clatter out an East German News Agency communique from other Warsaw Pact countries requesting the government to 'establish order' along the border. This meant the curbing of the 'unstable elements' who were being made to leave their homeland through 'deceit, bribery and blackmail'. The rights of the Western Allies in West Berlin, it was emphasised, would not be affected.

At thirty-five minutes past midnight armoured cars rolled into the Potsdamer Platz in the centre of Berlin where the American, British and Soviet sectors met. Soviet troops throughout the Eastern Zone also moved out of their barracks to dominate strategic positions throughout the whole country. By two-thirty the entire twenty-eight miles separating the Soviet Sector from the three Western sectors had been sealed, bar a few crossing points. It was hardly much of an obstacle at this stage – double strands of barbed wire held in place by a few posts – but it was enough to show the Berliners when they awoke in the morning that their city had been cut in two.

There was no reaction at all from the military headquarters in West Berlin. Though the right of free transit was guaranteed by four-power agreement, it had for so long been accepted by the West that the stream of refugees would be cut off that there seemed no occasion for surprise.

For the whole of 13th August there was no reaction, either, from Washington, London or Paris. Indeed, there was an almost audible sigh of relief along the corridors of Western power that a dangerous source of tension had been removed. In Britain the Foreign Secretary Sir Alec Douglas-Home was away from London shooting grouse and Prime Minister Harold MacMillan was holidaying in Scotland. When the US Secretary of State Dean Rusk released a comment late in the afternoon he merely confirmed that the new situation existed, only adding as an afterthought that the East German action

was a violation of the four-power status of Berlin. Though he thereby admitted that the East German action was illegal, he did not demand that the building of the wall be halted or that it be removed.

The Berliners themselves saw matters in a more serious light, Eastern Zone people as well as West. Several East German border patrolmen revolted at what they were doing to their own city. One of them was Sergeant Rudi Thurow, who later escaped and whose account gives an interesting insight into the reactions of an ordinary man to the task he was asked to perform. Thurow was on duty at 4am at the Bernau Station crossing-point when the first Eastern Zone Germans employed in the West arrived to cross the border to work. None of them had heard the news. Thurow had to tell them to turn back, and one called out '*Sei doch ein*

Armoured cars and East German militiamen take up positions

Mensch' – 'Show a little feeling'. Despite his shame, he was afraid to let anyone through in case he was informed against. Over and over again he repeated: 'Read the newspapers – they'll tell you all you need to know'. He heard one worker remark bitterly: 'I refuse to recognise this frontier if they are going to bar my way to my own mother. No-one can expect me to do a thing more for the state.' At breakfast time as the crowd grew around the station, and as its mood became more and more ugly, a party official approached Thurow and said 'Why don't you tell these people that this sealed border is an anti-fascist protective wall?' Thurow had indeed been told to use this phrase, but had not done so to avoid ridicule. Thurlow replied acidly: 'We don't need any instructions from people like you'. During the course of the morning, he felt more and more that the wall was unjust. Within the year, sixteen of his ninety-six-man company, including himself, had defected.

In West Berlin, reaction was led by the mayor, Willy Brandt, who went the rounds of the military authorities and told them in no uncertain terms that the Allied position on Berlin was at stake. East Germany had unilaterally destroyed the four-power status of the city. It was a blatant act of aggression which demanded an immediate show of force.

For most West Berliners, the closing of the border was indeed a disaster. Besides seperating them from friends and families, it meant that Berlin's main role – as they saw it – was at an end. No more could Eastern Sector inhabitants make a ready comparison between their own and a Western and capitalist society. No longer could Ulbricht be so easily weighed in the balance by ordinary people and found wanting. Communism could now consolidate its grip on East Germany.

With all these considerations in mind they waited for Western intervention, confident that the response would be as ready and as straight-forward as it had been in 1948. Meanwhile thousands of them gathered along the straggling wire frontier and many, using their identity cards, drove over into East Berlin to see what was happening for themselves.

East Berlin had become an armed camp. Russian-made tanks lined Unter den Linden and the Potsdamer Platz. Field kitchens and bivouac areas straddled streets. At 10.30 in the evening a crowd of 5,000 gathered before the Brandenburg Gate, their tempers on edge. All day long they had seen the barricade grow thicker, as reel after reel of barbed wire spiralled out to be added to the first flimsy obstacles. 'Hang Ulbricht!' they shouted, 'Put down your guns!' When eventually they retired to bed they were angry, perplexed and disappointed that nothing officially had been done to support them.

On Monday, the East Germans consolidated their position. They cut telephone and postal links, and West Berliners were ordered to remain one hundred metres from the barricade. Those who did not were sprayed with high-pressure hoses.

Still nothing from the West. At a diplomatic meeting at the State Department on Monday to draft the text of an official reaction, British and American representatives argued gravely against any rash actions which might upset the delicate balance in Berlin. A leak to the *Washington Evening Star* that day recorded only 'disapproval' as the government's reaction.

On Tuesday, the East Germans announced that West Berlin vehicles would no longer be allowed in the Eastern Sector without a special permit – a clear infringement of Western rights to unimpeded access. The same day, a young couple escaping across the Teltow Canal were fired on. They arrived safely, but it was a poor omen for the future.

Though a formal Allied protest was delivered that day, it merely recited

the events to date and protested against the measures only in the last paragraph. From Washington, the *New York Times* reported the Kennedy administration had 'decided to make a world-wide show of reasonableness'. It would do no more than portray the closure as 'a dramatic confession of Communist failure'.

To Berliners, such a reaction sounded completely cynical. One astonished official of the West Berlin government remarked that if the West won many more victories like that there would be nothing to defend in Berlin. By the evening, the mood in West Berlin was one of despair. The city's 13,000 riot police were put on full alert. Across the new frontier, forty-seven Russian-built T-34 tanks moved into position. At several points the barbed-wire barricades were replaced by concrete slabs.

The next day, Wednesday, liftable traffic barriers were placed at all the

East German troops erect barbed wire barricades

twelve remaining crossing points. That afternoon, a crowd of 250,000 people gathered at West Berlin's City Hall bearing signs protesting against the West's inaction. One read 'Munich 1938 – Berlin 1961,' another 'Paper Protests Don't Stop Tanks'.

There was little that Brandt could tell them, except to show that he understood their feelings. 'What happened here in the last three days,' he said, 'is a new version of the occupation of the Rhineland by Hitler. The man today is called Ulbricht.' The crowd dispersed, little reassured.

The demands which Brandt had made to the Allied commanders – and which he now repeated in a letter to Kennedy – were radical ones. They included Allied reinforcements, the deployment of a force along the frontier, the condemnation by the

West of the East German regime at the United Nations, the economic boycott of East German goods, the appointment of Lucius Clay, the hero of the airlift, as American commandant, the closure of the Communist Party Offices in West Berlin and a clamp-down on travel for East German officials.

For these demands, and for his efforts to involve Western politicians in the feelings of the Berliners he was roundly condemned in the US. Newspapers and politicians accused him of political trickery, geared to the coming West German elections, of being 'rude and presumptuous' for trying to tell Kennedy his job, of complicating the international situation unnecessarily, of being a 'mere mayor' who was 'trying to take over the foreign policy of the West'.

On Thursday some university students in Bonn sent Kennedy a black umbrella, symbolic of Neville Chamberlain whose policy of appeasement in 1938 paved the way for Hitler's dismemberment of Czechoslovakia. In Berlin, rail links between the two halves of the city were torn up by East German workmen, people in houses along the border were evacuated and windows facing West Berlin sealed up. Only on that evening, four whole days after the wall went up, did Kennedy express concern at the way things were going.

On Friday, he appointed Vice-President Lyndon Johnson and General Clay to a special mission to Berlin. It was also announced that there would be a strengthening in the US garrison in Berlin. 1,500 men would proceed in convoy down the autobahn from West Germany to emphasise that Western rights of access had not been affected. (At the same time, on the frontier, East German workmen began construction of a six-foot concrete wall which, according to their orders, had to be completed

Windows facing west are sealed up

along the entire length of the city division by Monday.)

Despite the delay, this was heartening news to the West Berliners, and when Johnson arrived at Tempelhof airport after lunch on Saturday he was greeted by a massive demonstration of relief. Standing by Brandt, Johnson told crowds: 'We remember your ordeals, we honour your fortitude, and we are with you in the determination to defend your liberty'. Despite a steady downpour, more than 400,000 people, many of them weeping openly, lined the route of the motorcade. A mile from Tempelhof, Johnson and Brandt stepped from their car and walked, moving slowly through the huge crowd, shaking myriads of hands as they went.

At City Hall stood another 300,000 people, and Johnson, himself now near tears, spoke again. He said nothing new and promised nothing, but his mere presence there was proof that Berlin's links with the free world were still strong. Next came Clay, who had a much stronger claim on the affection of the Berliners. He was, as Brandt reminded the crowds, the man who had saved the city in 1948. Again his words were no more than rhetoric,

Protesting crowds outside the West Berlin City Hall

though no less moving at that moment: 'Thanks to your courage and the support of my own countrymen and the support of all freedom-loving people, what we started together twelve years ago, we will finish together and Berlin will still be free'. The crowd cheered, the bands played *The Star Spangled Banner* and the *Deutschland Lied*, American and German flags waved damply from the City Hall tower, while from inside it the Freedom Bell, installed after the blockade, rang out a message of hope.

On Sunday, the reinforcements arrived to be greeted by Johnson himself and a crowd of thousands who pelted the trucks with bouquets of flowers. At last it was clear that the West intended to stay firm.

Could the West have stopped the Wall being built if such resolution had been shown initially? Certainly the East Germans had not expected it to be so easy; and a defecting border-guard later reported that, fearing a firm response and wishing not to escalate the crisis, the East German authorities had not supplied the troops with ammunition for their guns. Had tanks and bulldozers therefore flattened the puny fences at that stage, there would not have been much resistance.

But could the West have continued such a decisive line of action? It is unlikely. There was nothing to stop the East Germans building a second wall well inside their zonal boundary; to crush that, too, would have meant an Allied invasion of East Zone territory. This would have been as much a violation of Berlin's four-power status as the building of the wall itself, and would have been a direct threat to the Eastern Zone in a way that the wall itself did not threaten the Western Zone. The move would certainly have led to war.

Ultimately, unless the West was ready for war over Berlin, East Germany and Russia could exercise

Construction of the wall begins

their power to do as they liked in East Berlin, and if they cared to ignore existing agreements no-one was going to stop them. It was a situation, again, that had been implicit in the Russian decision to break up the four-power command structure of the city in 1946.

Far from wanting war, indeed, the West wanted detente and was ready in principle to accept such a solution to the Berlin problem. Provided the main rights in West Berlin remained secure: the rights of free access, the right to keep troops there, and the continued economic viability of Western sectors.

By hindsight, the wall was anyway inevitable sooner or later. Even if Brandt had had his way, even if the West had successfully protested at every attempted violation of the agreed rights from 1949 on and even if

A full alert of Western forces is ordered

148

Vice-President Johnson and Willy Brandt in Berlin

there had been no crisis fomented by Ulbricht and Khrushchev, the existence of West Berlin as an escape hatch for East Germans would in the long term have served the purpose of neither East Germany nor the West.

The existence of the open border was useful in political terms to Berlin and the West only in so far as it might one day have so weakened East Germany or put such political pressure on the regime that the way might have been opened for the reunification of Germany. In fact, such a thing was unthinkable: Russia would never have tolerated the collapse of her satellite. Had the frontier remained open therefore, East Germany would have remained a more repressive and poverty stricken place than it subsequently became – scarcely in the interests of either its government or its people. True, there was a moral question, and to West

Berliners this was understandably paramount: with the frontier closed, there was no chance of freedom for anyone on the other side. It was an aspect of the problem that was sadly ignored by the Western Allies, more concerned with longer-term, impersonal policy-making in the days of the period immediately following 13th August.

Johnson's visit retrieved the situation somewhat. It changed none of the facts but is was a hugely successful public relations exercise, restoring the city's confidence. And now that Kennedy understood the importance of an explicit commitment by the West, the Western response hardened considerably: when the East Germans issued a new decree banning West Berliners from approaching the wall within one hundred metres, the three Allied commandants ordered a full alert of Western forces and despatched 1,000 troops, backed up by tanks, to defend the territorial integrity of West Berlin up to the wall itself.

At the end of the month, Adenauer added to his demands for firmness with an astute political argument: unless the Americans stood firm, he told Kennedy, there was a real danger that Germany would embrace neutrality, withdraw from the Western Alliance and come to her own terms with Russia. As a result, Kennedy appointed Clay his personal representative in Berlin. It was the most powerful declaration he could make to Berliners, to Germans and to Russia that the West would brook no further infringement of its rights in Berlin.

In political terms, the Berliners were secure. But there was no such easy way to assuage the emotional insecurities to which they were subjected every day by the presence of the wall.

A British anti-tank gun near the Brandenburg Gate

The enduring wall

Tear gas drifts along the wall

The Berlin Wall remains a strangely ominous sight, zigzagging along the historical borough boundaries, cutting a wide barren swath through the city, allowing only skeletal watch-towers, searchlights and concrete columns to flourish. At its most sophisticated, it is a remarkable combination of devices. A would-be escapee could encounter in sequence an eight-foot fence, a barbed-wire entanglement, thin strips of electrified alarm wire, a canal, patrol dogs, mine fields, a death strip in which a person is shot on sight and raked sand to show up footprints and all this swept by searchlights at night. Should he successfully negotiate these obsta-

cles, which have been tested against the resources of East Germany's finest athletes, he would be faced with the wall itself, perhaps twelve feet high and surmounted by spikes, barbed wire or, in some places, enormous concrete cylinders placed horizontally so that they will roll off and crush anyone who seizes them.

To motor along the wall – on either side – is a strange experience. On the West, gaunt concrete slabs give way constantly to black-windowed housefronts which form much of the structure; it looms up suddenly and just as quickly disappears at right angles, only to confront one again almost at once sitting squarely across a dead-end road. In the East, it often looks a strangely gimcrack structure, shored up by iron or wood supports that loose themselves in a cluster of tank-traps and barbed-wire at its base.

Despite all precautions, however, there have been many escapes, some of which are now legendary. 500 of the escapees have been army guards, who from the beginning have paraded in pairs or threes so as to keep an eye on each other. One guard disabled the sub-machine guns in his watchtower, and then clambered to safety in full view of his helpless colleagues. On another occasion police in the West spotted two East German guards signalling that they were about to make a dash for the border. The Western police took cover, preparing to return fire if any shots crossed the border. The two East Germans then dashed for the barbed wire, swinging at it with their guns, while machine-gun fire from a watchtower 300 yards away kicked up the ground around them. A couple of bursts from the West aimed above the watchtowers gave them the time they needed to make it to safety.

There have been several cases of extreme callousness displayed by the East Germans towards escapees, and these still rankle with West Berliners. On 13th December 1963 a twenty-four-

Some of the obstacles facing the would-be escapee

year-old man, Dieter Berger, was discovered to be escaping by the guards. He turned back to surrender, but despite this being his obvious intention he was shot down – and the guards continued to shoot as he crawled wounded towards them. Berger died later in hospital and two guards were awarded medals for 'meritorious achievement'.

One of the most famous escape attempts occurred in the early afternoon of 17th August 1962, when two eighteen-year-olds tried to cross the wall near Checkpoint Charlie. One got clear, but the other, Peter Fechter, was hit. He lay slowly bleeding to death within full view of both East Berlin guards and angry West Berliners. The guards made no move to help him, despite Fechter's repeated agonised pleas for help. West Berlin police threw him bandages, but he was too weak to reach them.

After an hour, the guards set up a smoke screen and dragged him back into the Eastern Sector. Reaction in West Berlin mounted to hysteria as accusations were thrown at police and troops for not themselves dragging Fechter to safety.

Another well known incident occurred on 14th March 1966, when East German guards wounded and captured two would-be escapees. The two later died in hospital, and it emerged they had both been children, one aged thirteen the other ten. More events occurred in January 1967 to horrify the West. Two escapees were killed after they had reached West Berlin territory. The two tried to swim the Teltow Canal at a spot where both banks of the canal are in the Western Sector. They successfully negotiated the wall itself, but guards pursued them on to the towpath, wounded one man who dived into the water and never reappeared, and shot the other when he was almost at the far bank. This man had just called out

dived into the water, from which she was dragged to safety, shivering and shocked, but otherwise unhurt.

Many escape tunnels have been built and many discovered, flooded or walled up. Numbers of lives have been lost when walls have fallen in and water mains have broken, and many have been shot trying to gain the entrance to some escape route. Many, however, have crawled to safety beneath the feet of the Vopos – the *Volkspolizei* (People's Police).

The best known of the tunnels was the one begun in May 1962, planned and financed largely by the Berlin staff of the American TV company,

to some workmen, who were preparing to offer him the end of a pole to help him out when they were sent to cover by the shooting, and when they returned the refugee had sunk.

There are, fortunately, many escape stories with happy endings. On 21st September 1965 a young typist from Leipzig, named Ursula, who had fallen in love with a Frenchman and was desperate to join him in the West, slipped unobserved on. to a barge loaded with sand for West Berlin, and hid under a tarpaulin. She went through the checkpoints undiscovered, but was spotted by the captain and his wife as she peeped out to see if she had arrived safely in the West. West Berlin workmen and customs guards watched anxiously as she was seized, struggled free and

The body of Peter Fechter, a youth shot by East Berlin guards while attempting to escape with a companion. The incident provoked very violent reaction among West Berliners

Repairs to the wall.
Two young East Berliners crashed
through at this point in a truck and
successfully reached the West

NBC. It was started in an unused
workshop on the Bernauer Strasse,
where small Volkswagen buses went
in and out unsuspected, bringing
electrical tools, lumber, and other
things needed for the work. The
tunneling itself was done by some
fifty young men working in shifts for
a period of six months.

The initial shaft was fifteen feet
deep and took three nights to dig and
make safe. Then the workers, crouch-
ing in muddy water, began pulling
the earth out in little containers for
which they laid a track. A single
electric bulb gave dim light, and the
workers were in constant danger of
cave-ins until they built a wooden
frame with a supporting ceiling to
lessen the risk. Through June and
July, the tunnel edged forward until
it stretched over 400 feet towards
West Berlin.

The Vopos were constantly pat-
rolling up above, and keeping an
especially careful watch at Bernauer
Strasse, a frequently used escapee
jumping off point. Their pacing could
be heard by the men working far under

youth with a West German passport who had been permitted to cross at Checkpoint Charlie. The first twenty-eight people crawled to safety; babies and children were dragged along in the tin basins that had been used for bringing out the earth. Trembling and sometimes in tears, but still silent in order not to betray the escape route, they were restored with hot coffee.

A second crossing and a third were carried out at short intervals, but with each episode and with more people being involved, the danger of

Jump to freedom

the pavement and there was no talking in the tunnel for fear of the East German police hearing.

The long task was not over until October. During those months dozens of shorter tunnels had been dug; some had been discovered and blocked up, some had caved in. Some of the escapees had collapsed in the narrow tunnels, some, wounded before their escape, had died after they reached the West. Methods used to detect tunnelling constantly improved, and tunnel digging became constantly more perilous.

In mid-October a few people assembled in the cellar, alerted by a

Volkspolizei **inspecting the entrance of a tunnel**

discovery increased. Too many on both sides of the wall knew of the operation. In all, fifty-nine persons had used the tunnel to escape by late October, when the increasing risk forced the leaders to flood the shaft.

The tunnel was a remarkable story in another way: NBC was, for a price, permitted to film the construction and the escape. Its ninety-minute documentary was seen by millions – but only after the possibility of using the tunnel was over and with the knowledge that the East German authorities had already perfected the listening devices and electronic equipment necessary to detect such activities.

No-one knows how many have escaped over the wall – several thousand certainly – and some seventy have died in their attempts.

But the incentive to escape is lessening – ironically as a result of the building of the wall, which at first seemed to have turned East Germany into a prison. For the wall, by slowing the West-bound flood to a trickle, allowed East Germany to rebuild her shattered economy until now her industrial power rivals that of the West; it allowed a consolidation of power in Eastern Europe; and by firmly blocking any chance of reunification, it opened the way to Willy Brandt's successful Eastern policy of recognition and reconciliation with Russia and her satellites.

Thus, by a round-about route, the wall has led to a radical improvement in relations between the two Germanies, now dealing with each other as fully-fledged nations. It may be that in the not too far distant future the contacts severed by the establishment of East Germany and the building of the wall will be remade on a new basis. Perhaps one day, the building of the wall will be regarded as good an investment by the West as it is by the East.

A few of the thousands who succeeded in their attempts to cross to the West